SMART WORKING

LIFESKILLS INTERNATIONAL LTD

Lifeskills team of writers:
Barrie Hopson
Jack Loughary
Steve Murgatroyd
Teresa Ripley
Mike Scally
Don Simpson

Lifeskills Series Editor: Jonathan Kitching

Gower

Published by
Gower Publishing Limited
Gower House
Croft Road
Aldershot
Hampshire GU11 3HR

Gower
Old Post Road
Brookfield
Vermont 05036
USA

Lifeskills International Ltd have asserted their rights under the Copyright, Designs and Patents Act 1988 to be identified as the proprietors of this work.

British Library Cataloguing in Publication Data
Smart working
    1.Management
    I.Hopson, Barrie, 1943-
    658.4

    ISBN 0 566 08143 1

Typeset in Middlesex by SetPoint and printed in the United Kingdom at the University Press, Cambridge

Contents

PREFACE

How many times do we hear, or use, the statement: 'It's not about working harder, but working smarter'?

Managers in today's organizations have the challenge of merging management systems that incorporate traditional human values with efficiency-oriented technology. *Smart Working* takes up this challenge in three basic areas: time management and life satisfaction; interpersonal communications; and group communications.

Part I, Time Management and Life Satisfaction, not only encompasses important techniques for making productive use of work time, but also extends its focus to using non-work time to gain maximum life satisfaction. Because work, family, personal, leisure and other non-work goals often overlap, there is value in considering them as components of the larger picture of life satisfaction, as a foundation for the techniques of time and activity planning. Chapter 1, Your Starting Point – the Basics of Time Management, is an introduction and review of well-tested time-management techniques. Chapter 2, Beyond the Basics, extends the concern beyond work to other selected applications of time management.

Part I is based on the premise that in order to manage others productively, a manager must be able to manage him- or herself both on and off the job. Selections from Lifeskills' successful publications concerned with time management, goal setting, personal diaries and leisure are included. Attention is given to both concepts and techniques of personal management. Even though there are many ways to manage time efficiently, employees are more likely to accord importance to managing their own time effectively if they see their managers as desirable role models.

If there is general agreement on any single area of management competencies, it is probably on interpersonal communication. More than one communication researcher has concluded that if we are lucky, we can communicate accurately about 50 per cent of what we mean, and understand clearly about 50 per cent of what we hear. Getting ahead of those odds is a task that successful managers work at on a daily basis. Fortunately, effective communication is more than just good luck.

There are a variety of techniques and concepts that can enhance how well we communicate with others. Part II of the book begins with Chapter 3, Straight Talk, which reviews basic communication skills. Chapter 4, More than Talk, includes discussion of non-verbal aspects of communication, so important to the work of managers, as well as dealing with employee conflict and feedback techniques in communication. It includes instructions for practising specific communication skills and procedures involved in management tasks.

Communication in group settings is the focus of Part III of the book. Chapter 5, Making Meetings Work, is concerned with producing effective staff meetings via clear communication. Chapter 6, Some Further Thoughts – Making Sense of Group Behaviour, takes a broader view of the topic of groups and also looks more specifically at productive and not so productive verbal behaviours in working groups. The chapter discusses group development and principles for organizing and managing groups.

Smart Working is for people who care about personal development. It involves reading and doing, so we have written it in an open learning format. Open learning describes a study programme that is designed so that it adapts to the needs of individual learners. This means that throughout the book the reader is invited to interact with the text.

'Reader interaction boxes' help the individual to personalize the contents of the book to particular situations and interests and also facilitate thought about the material presented. Research has shown that these techniques can enhance one's understanding and application of the material. These boxes usually include questions about the material being read. In addition, the reader should feel free to write notes, comments and questions wherever they choose in the book. Open learning is all about being involved with the ideas and concepts and being active in one's learning.

Some open learning programmes involve attendance at a study centre of some kind, or contact with a tutor or mentor, but even then attendance times are flexible and suit the individual. This book is for you to use at home or at work. Most of the activities are for you to complete on your own. Sometimes we may suggest that you talk with a friend or colleague, because self-development is easier if there is another person with whom to talk over ideas. However, this isn't essential by any means.

With this book you can:

♦ organize your study to suit your own needs
♦ study the material alone or with other people
♦ work through the material at your own pace
♦ start and finish when and where you want to.

Some sections involve you in more than working through the text; they require you to take additional time – sometimes an evening, sometimes a week. For this reason, we do not suggest specifically how long it will take you to work through this book, but the written part of it will probably take about six hours to complete.

PART I

TIME MANAGEMENT AND LIFE SATISFACTION

Part I of this book is about using your time to maximize your life satisfaction. The idea of time as a quantity that can be managed makes sense and has a natural-sounding appeal, but in the long run it is what each one of us does within the allotted time we have that makes a difference to the quality of our lives. A useful way to understand that idea is to be clear about how, as a manager, you use various blocks of time to accomplish the tasks for which you have assumed responsibility. The two chapters in Part I address both conceptual and practical aspects of time management, and move on from work time to consider leisure time.

The case for the importance of managing work time has been made by many writers over the years. There is an equally appealing case for the satisfying use of the busy manager's leisure time. The demands on many, if not most, managers can be intense, so much so that time originally reserved for non-work activities is gradually given over to work. The situation is considered serious and can be unhealthy, as suggested by the frequently used term 'workaholic'. The old warning 'All work and no play makes for a dull whoever' applies here. Many workaholics probably believe that they are excellent time managers and, from the perspective of squeezing every drop of production out of every moment, they may be correct. The question, put bluntly perhaps, is often: 'So what?' If being busy for busyness's sake is what motivates you, then the issue may be more one of values and time awareness than of time management.

Time awareness is one of the paramount issues in Part I. It is important to be aware of one's values and to allot time and energy consistently with them. Time is viewed as a resource and, like any other resource, it is wise to account for its use. The topics of list making, setting time priorities and analysing satisfaction derived from different kinds of activity are treated in an interactive manner in Chapter 1; that is, you are invited to use your own time records to assist in understanding the concepts discussed.

This recording work needs to take place for at least one week, before moving on to the materials that follow.

Chapter 2, Beyond the Basics, covers techniques for the use of time such as keeping diaries and creating work environments that support time budgets, as well as several time savers. Consideration is also given to helping ensure that you also achieve time for satisfying leisure. The latter is not an easy task for many managers, who seem continually to be faced with more demands than time permits. As you read and complete the exercises in both chapters you should develop your competency to become more in charge of your time, using it to achieve the goals in life that you cherish most.

The objectives of Part I, therefore, are to help you to:

◆ become aware of how you presently use your time
◆ prioritize the ways in which you use your time
◆ rank your priorities in order of importance
◆ explore the concepts of sold time, maintenance time and discretionary time
◆ develop your skills in managing time.

The important skill that Part I of this book emphasizes is the ability to establish priorities and to apportion time to achieve them. It offers you the opportunity to explore techniques for planning your time more effectively so that you can accomplish all your important priorities, some of your less important priorities, and even a few of the relatively unimportant ones.

We realize that life is full of unexpected surprises, so another important element in this programme is flexibility. Indeed, this book itself is flexible, in that you choose when and how you use it. By the time you have reached the end of Part I, we hope that you will be able to choose and use your time more efficiently and will no longer think, 'I would like to do that but I haven't got the time'. Instead, you will either arrange to do it or think, 'I could do that, but I like what I'm doing a lot better'.

What do you want to get out of this section of the book? Before you move on, take about five minutes to reflect on what you would like to achieve.

Make a note of three things you find frustrating about the way you currently spend your time. For example, are you often late? Do you find it difficult to get certain things done? Do you feel that all your time belongs to other people?

Now let your imagination loose for a few minutes to think about the possibilities that you could open up for yourself.

What are your personal objectives in completing this section of the book?

What important thing would you really like to achieve that you don't have time for currently?

What two things would you like to change about the way you spend your time?

Now that you have begun to identify your personal goals, we suggest that you keep returning to these as you work through the materials. Reviewing your objectives regularly will help you monitor your progress. It will also help you choose the time-management techniques that are most helpful to you. As you work, don't hesitate to change or add to your objectives; your ideas will change along with your progress!

1

YOUR STARTING POINT - THE BASICS OF TIME MANAGEMENT

What is time management? It involves setting clear priorities for yourself and making sure that you achieve them. Time is a limited resource, so you have to make choices. When the time is gone, it's gone. It's worth learning how to conquer the clock now!

Three key words can help you achieve better management of your time:

◆ *Knowledge* – a clear recognition of what you need or want to do
◆ *Choice* – the need to make a choice from among the alternatives
◆ *Time* – the need to schedule time to act on your choice.

Managing time does not mean always being busy. We are not suggesting that every minute must be packed with activity, but rather that it is possible to get what you want out of as much time as you have. That includes planning for relaxation (see Figure 1.1).

We each have 24 hours available every day. We can regard them as we would an investment; where and how you invest them determines what you get in return from the day. The first step in time management is knowing how you really spend your time. You can do this by completing the time investment record, which lists your activities throughout the week. This will provide you with the basic information that will help you to make choices about time later on. The objective of this chapter is therefore to help you to become aware of how you actually spend your time.

Time management is about priorities

Priorities result from setting objectives

Setting objectives is about planning

Planning is about control

Being in control is being self-empowered

Self-empowered people manage their time

Figure 1.1 *Time management flowchart*

Time investment record

The time investment record in Table 1.1 splits the days of the week into two-hour periods. We suggest that you fill in the record over the next seven consecutive days.

We have found that recording your time in two-hour blocks is effective, but you can split the chart into whatever time periods suit you, although these should not be too long. Every night, enter into the record what you did during the day. It is important to make your entries regularly each day, because it is easy to forget what you have done. You will need to complete a full week (seven 24-hour periods) of time investment records before you can proceed with the rest of the programme.

You may find it helpful to keep a log, jotting down things as you do them during the day. You will still need to transfer your entries into the time investment record at the end of the week to provide an overview of how you spent your time. An overview is very important, as it will allow you to look back and identify time-use patterns. When you have completed your time investment record for a week, you will be able to analyse how your time was spent.

Table 1.1 *Time investment record*

	Mon	Tue	Wed	Thu	Fri	Sat	Sun
AM 12–2							
2–4							
4–6							
6–8							
8–10							
10–12							
PM 12–2							
2–4							
4–6							
6–8							
8–10							
10–12							

In the time activity chart in Table 1.2, list the activities described in your time investment record (for example sleeping, eating, caring for children, watching television, shopping, cooking, domestic tasks, driving or being at work). You may find it useful to break down how you spend your time at work. Use subheadings for your different work activities (for example, telephone calls, attending meetings or travelling).

Table 1.2 *Time activity chart*

Activity	Number of hours spent
Eating	
Childcare	
Sleeping	
Travelling	
Shopping	
Domestic chores	
Cooking	
Working	
Others	

Next, calculate out how many hours you spent on each activity. Enter this figure in the space provided to the right of the activity.

Spend a few minutes looking over your chart. Then rank your activities using the rank order activity chart in Table 1.3.

Table 1.3 *Rank order activity chart*

Activity	Number of hours spent
1	
2	
3	
4	
5	
6	
7	
8	
9	
10	
11	
12	
13	
14	
15	
16	
17	
18	
19	
20	

Put the activity you spend most time on next to 1, the next most time consuming next to 2 and so on.

Look over your chart and consider the following.

What, if anything, surprises you about the way you have spent your week?

_____

_____

Was there anything unusual about this particular week?

_____

_____

What return are you getting on your investment; that is, how satisfied are you in general and with particular activities?

What changes would you like to make?

Can you see ways to save time so that you could invest it in something else? If so, what are they?

You now have an analysis of how you actually spent a week of your life. It may have produced some surprises for you! For example, the amount of time spent watching television or walking the dog might be much greater than you thought. Maybe you spent less time on the briefcase full of 'homework' than you had thought. Even if your time investment record turned out as you expected, it will be worth considering whether the full picture has the balance and variety that you desire. You will never have that week again.

Are you happy about the ways in which you spent your time? In Chapter 2 you will be asked to look at your time investment record in more detail, so that you can start identifying areas where you might save time or put it to better use.

Reflecting further on that week and how representative it was, ask yourself the following questions to review your use of time last week.

What are my overall impressions of how I spent the week and how I spend my time generally?

How much time have I given, and do I give generally, to what I enjoy?

How much time have I spent, and do I spend, on what I don't enjoy?

Have I wasted time? How much? How?

How much time was given, and do I give generally, to what I think is important?

Did I make constructive use of any time I spent waiting or travelling?

How much time did I, and do I generally, allocate to my priorities?

_____

Did I go into each day knowing what I wanted to achieve?

_____

Did anything that I wanted to do get postponed?

_____

Have I used any time particularly successfully this week?

_____

Have I spent time on routines or habits that I would like to break?

_____

Have I rewarded myself for time well spent?

_____

Have I set some deadlines for myself and met them?

_____

_____

Have I wasted other people's time at all? If so, how?

_____

_____

Have I found, and do I generally find, time to relax?

_____

_____

Have I frequently asked myself, 'What is the best use of my time right now?'

_____

_____

What do my answers tell me about how I used my time last week?

_____

_____

It will help to continue doing a time-check review every week. We have included a sample daily time chart (Table 1.4) to indicate things you might include. This chart is especially helpful in recording work-based activity, but it's also useful to include time spent outside working hours.

Table 1.4 *Daily time chart*

Time	Activity
8.50	*Cup of tea. Searched for missing letters. Did some filing too.*
9.25	*Couple of people wanting to talk.*
9.35	*Begin meeting with Mike on posters to accompany a book. It's hard to decide what we want.*
10.05	*Typesetter arrives. We all three look at boards.*
10.35	*Publishing team meeting, followed by debriefing session with MD.*
11.50	*Cup of coffee. Chat with Ann Marie. Karen ill so sent her home!*
12.30	*Back to poster meeting and reading typeset boards.*
1.00	*Continue poster concept meeting at lunch.*
1.45	*Pick up boards again.*
2.15	*Barrie telephoned; leaving messages etc.*
2.35	*Glanced through two magazines (HRD Quarterly, Training Tomorrow).*
2.50	*Photocopy our drafts and ideas for poster. Start layout.*
3.50	*Designs for new catalogue cover arrive. Peter, Michael and I look at them.*
4.05	*Mike briefs me on publication schedule of NOW books.*
4.30	*Make two phone calls. Get together to celebrate two birthdays.*
5.00	*Return to layout for 20 minutes. Write out tasks for tomorrow.*
5.45	*Leave office.*

You may find that by keeping your daily time charts together, you are better able to review your progress and identify recurring features. Later, we will look at the techniques of using a time-management personal planner.

So far, you have begun to think about how you really use your time. You will now be asked to go into more detail and find out how to plan to use more time for the things you enjoy.

Time and satisfaction

Let's turn now to the central problem in time management – how well we match what we want to do with what we actually do. The aim is to increase the time we spend on satisfying activities as a proportion of all time spent. To do this, we need to know how we actually spend our time now, how satisfying that is and how we might spend our time differently in order to give ourselves greater satisfaction and pleasure. Let's look at a technique for doing this.

Satisfying activities

Make a list of the activities in your present use of time that satisfy you. Define satisfaction in your own terms, but include only those activities that you are actually involved in currently. Make your list one that shows what actually satisfies you, not what you think it 'ought to be'.

Now transfer the information on that list to a pie chart in a way that shows the activities you get the most satisfaction from and those that yield the least. A pie chart can identify the activities that satisfy you and the relative satisfaction you get from each activity by causing you to think proportionately. Everyone's 'satisfaction pie' is different. Examine the two different examples in Figures 1.2 and 1.3; your pie chart will probably contain many activities that are different from these examples.

Now enter your own satisfying activities on the blank pie chart that follows as Figure 1.4, with each activity as a slice of the pie. The more satisfying the activity, the larger its slice of the pie. The complete pie is a synopsis of your satisfying life activities.

One point the pie chart makes clear is that you can increase the time you devote to one satisfying activity only at the expense of time devoted to another activity. This means that you have to make choices, to reduce time spent on less satisfying

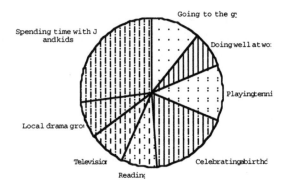

Figure 1.2 *Jane's satisfaction pie*

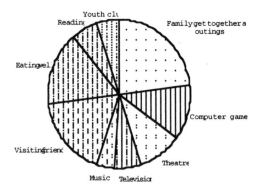

Figure 1.3 *Eric's satisfaction pie*

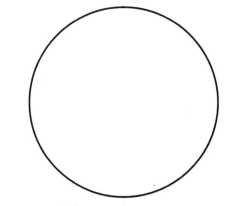

Figure 1.4 *Your satisfaction pie*

activities in order to increase the time available for more attractive activities.

Spend a minute or two looking at your satisfaction pie. Then go on to the next stage, which looks at the amount of time you actually spend on each of your satisfying activities.

Time spent on satisfying activities

We have shown you Jane's and Eric's satisfaction pies and in Figures 1.5 and 1.6 are their 'actual-time pies'. As you can see, there are discrepancies. For example, like many of us, they both watch more television than the satisfaction they get from that activity warrants!

On the blank actual-time pie in Figure 1.7, enter the amount of time you now spend on your satisfying activities. This time, the size of the slice indicates the actual amount of time spent in proportion to other activities.

Compare your two pies, the time spent against satisfaction gained, and consider these questions.

Does anything surprise you about either of your pies?

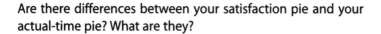

_____

Are there differences between your satisfaction pie and your actual-time pie? What are they?

_____

What does this say about your current lifestyle and use of time?

_____

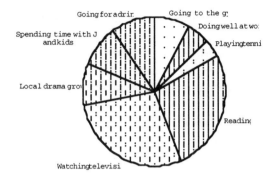

Figure 1.5 *Jane's actual-time pie*

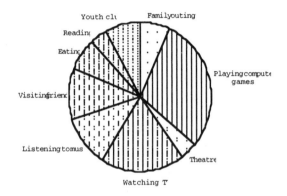

Figure 1.6 *Eric's actual-time pie*

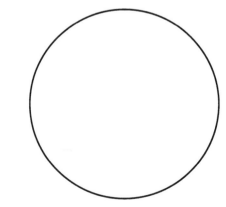

Figure 1.7 *Your actual-time pie*

Look again at the example pies. Many of the things that Jane and Eric really enjoy and find satisfying are squeezed out by other activities. Now look now again at your time investment record and compare it with your satisfaction and actual-time pies. Reflect on the following two questions.

Are there any other satisfying activities in your time investment record that are not included in your satisfaction pie?

Your actual-time pie shows the amount of time you think you spend on satisfying activities. Your time investment record shows the amount of time you actually spend on all activities over one week. If you think in terms of a return on your investment (satisfaction), what shifts might you begin to make in your use of time?

We have been asking you to focus on activities that you do now that you find satisfying. Now use your imagination! In an ideal world, how would you spend your time? Overleaf you will find a final pair of pies. Using the same headings as in your original two pies, fill in the satisfaction pie as you would like it to look and the actual-time pie as you would like it to look.

By comparing your actual and your ideal sets of pies, you now know where you are and where you would like to be. You have the basic information for making time-management decisions that will enable you to manage your time to your greater satisfaction. Today is the first day of the rest of your life, so make the most of it!

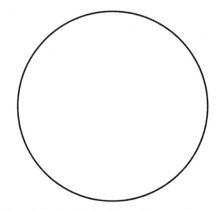

Figure 1.8 *Your ideal satisfaction pie*

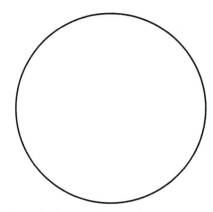

Figure 1.9 *Your ideal actual-time pie*

Sold time, maintenance time and discretionary time

Not all of our time is free for us to shape. It can be helpful to think in terms of 'sold time', 'maintenance time' and 'discretionary time'. (This classification of time was developed by Jack Loughary of the University of Oregon.)

Sold time is that which we sell to an employer or, if we are a student, the time spent studying. It involves exchanging our time for money or for qualifications, which can be regarded as future money. Sold time extends beyond the actual hours spent at work or in education. It includes the time spent organizing or preparing for these, travelling, homeworking and so on.

Maintenance time is the time spent keeping our lives in workable order. It is time spent on the tasks that are necessary to maintain ourselves – eating and sleeping, for example. It also includes time spent maintaining others, cooking and cleaning, shopping, caring for family members and so on.

Discretionary time is the time that remains. This is when we can choose how we want to spend our time.

Review your time investment record using the sold time, maintenance time and discretionary time charts in Tables 1.5–1.7. Fill each one in for last week, using your time investment record if necessary. You will find that some activities are difficult to categorize. For example, cooking, bathing the children or shopping could all be maintenance time or discretionary time; it depends on whether or not you enjoy the activity and have chosen to do it.

Under each type of time, record your activities that fall into each category. Write down the amount of time you spend on each activity for each day of the week. Calculate the daily total for each type of time and enter this figure in the 'Total' line at the bottom of each chart. Then, add up the grand total for each type of time.

You should now have a clear picture of your daily totals for the three different categories of time, and a weekly total for each. On the next few pages are examples of how one user's charts looked.

If possible, persuade some of your friends or colleagues to complete time charts so that you can compare them with yours. People live their lives very differently. There is no right or wrong pattern. However, within individual patterns there usually is some room for adjustment. Where this is possible, most of us would choose to increase discretionary time, because that is the time where we can choose what we really want to do and possibly, of course, increase our life satisfaction.

Table 1.5 *Sold time chart*

	Mon	Tue	Wed	Thu	Fri	Sat	Sun		
Total									Grand total

Table 1.6 *Maintenance time chart*

Mon	Tue	Wed	Thu	Fri	Sat	Sun		
								Grand total

Total

Table 1.7 Discretionary time chart

	Mon	Tue	Wed	Thu	Fri	Sat	Sun
Total							
Grand total							

Table 1.8 *Michael's sold time chart*

	Mon	Tue	Wed	Thu	Fri	Sat	Sun
	7.40 Travel to work 8.30–5.30 Work Travel home, 40 mins Work at home, 1 hour	7.30–8.30 Work (inc. travel time)	7.30–5.45 Work plus travel (40 mins) Work at home, 1 hour	7.30–5.20 Working, travel home, 40 mins	7.30–5.40 Work inc. travel home		
Total	11.50	13.00	11.50	10.30	10.10	None	None
						Grand total	57.20

Table 1.9 Michael's maintenance time chart

	Mon	Tue	Wed	Thu	Fri	Sat	Sun
	7, got up, get ready, 20 mins Breakfast, 15 mins Bed, 10pm	6.30 got up, get ready, 1 hour No evening meal – big lunch Bed, 9pm	7, got up, get ready, 35 mins Shopping in evening, 1 hour Bed, 9pm	3.30–7.30 get ready, go to work Get ready to go out, 6.50–7.30 Bed, 12 midnight	7, got up Evening meal, 1 hour Bed, 10.30pm	9am, got up Bath, 10.30 Lunch, 1.5 hours Dinner, 1 hour Bed, 10.30 pm	10.30 got up Brunch, 1 hour Clean car, 1 hour Cook and eat meal, 1.75 hrs Bed, 11pm
Total	10.05	9.30	11.35	11.00	8.00	14.30	16.45
						Grand total	81.25

Table 1.10 *Michael's discretionary time chart*

	Mon	Tue	Wed	Thu	Fri	Sat	Sun
	Out for evening meal, 2 hours	TV, 30 mins	Talked and drank at home, 1.5 hours	Went out for meal, 4.5 hours	Records, 1.5 hours TV, coffee, 1 hour Guitar, 20 mins Write letters, 1hr 20 mins	Holiday prep, 1.5 hours Buy gifts, 3 hours Assemble VCR, 1.5 hours DIY kit, 4 hours	Holiday decor and food, 3 hours Make fire, 0.5 hrs Parents visit, 1.5 hours Read, 1.5 hours
Total	2.00	0.30	1.30	4.30	6.10	9.00	6.30
						Grand total	30.10

Reflect on your three time charts. Are there any changes you might make in your sold and maintenance time to increase your discretionary time? Make a note of any ideas.

An increase in discretionary time obviously requires a reduction in maintenance time and sold time. We could choose to neglect any active, physical exercise time to have more time for conversation or reading, but this could be unwise or unacceptable. One way of increasing discretionary time is by performing our sold time and maintenance time activities more efficiently – that is, in less time – and also to be clear about 'time cheaters' and 'time beaters'. With an understanding of these, you should have more time to do the things you want. We will look at time cheaters and time beaters at a later stage.

Identifying priorities

We have only 24 hours in a day. Time is finite, but the possible demands on it are infinite. If we are not simply to react to demands, we must choose how to allocate our time or, in other words, identify priorities. You have analysed how you spent your time last week. Now you can consider how you plan to spend your time next week.

Creating a priorities chart

Record all the ideas that occur to you in response to the following two headings. You will probably spend about three minutes on each topic. Put your answers in any order; simply note your ideas freely as they occur to you.

What I have to do next week:

_____

_____

What I want to do next week:

_____

_____

Take each set of ideas in turn and pick out the most important items that you have to do or want to do next week.

When you have done this, look over the items that you have selected. Ask yourself which of the activities you are going to give the most priority to. Think through all the factors, the implications of making a particular item your priority. Work on the pros and cons of making each item a priority and then decide which will be your number-one choice. List your choices in order of priority.

Priorities for this week:

_____

_____

Now that you have created your list of priorities, you may find it helpful to place a copy where you will see it frequently during

the next week. Review the list two or three times during the week and strike through items as you complete them. What is left undone on the list at the end of the week can be included in the priorities you set for the following week.

At the end of the next week, review your list of priorities and then answer the following questions. If you find it helpful, talk through with a friend or colleague how you found this experience of clarifying the priorities which can shape your week.

How aware were you of your priorities as the week progressed?

_____

_____

How much are you choosing/initiating?

_____

_____

Are you proactive or reactive? (Do you make things happen or are you inclined to let things happen to you?)

_____

_____

We have looked at the principle of identifying priorities and have begun to explore techniques for doing this. In the next chapter, we will look at another useful technique for ranking priorities in order of importance.

2

Beyond the Basics

This chapter builds on the basic time-management work you accomplished in the previous one. It includes a consideration of time diaries and planners. These are valuable management tools and are now available in electronic formats, including hand-held, laptop and desktop models. The basic concepts discussed in this chapter are valid for whatever medium you might choose. Your choice should be based on the kind and amount of information to be used and your style of working.

Your personal information base obviously varies a great deal with the level and kind of management functions for which you have responsibility. A good rule of thumb is: begin with a traditional manual diary system if you want to gain experience of how a time-management tool can affect your work. Changing to an electronic system is not a difficult transition for most people when the need arises.

The chapter also invites you to consider leisure and other non-work interests as part of time management. If you haven't examined these values in conjunction with those of work, this is a good time to do so. A basic point of the chapter is that leisure and personal values, just like work responsibilities, can benefit from thoughtful, systematic consideration.

Effective list making

We all have important things to do in our lives, but how do we remember how and when to do them? Trusting to memory is one way but, unfortunately, it is not very reliable. Indeed, trying to remember long lists of things to do can in itself be stressful. Relying on someone else to remind you of things means handing over responsibility for your life to someone else, which is not very self-empowered behaviour! One satisfactory way of guaranteeing that you achieve your priorities is by effective list making.

Some people believe that list making is tedious and is a way of wasting time rather than saving it. Weigh up the advantages and disadvantages of list making for yourself – if you don't make lists already, try it and see. We've suggested some advantages, but there is an opportunity to add some of your own. Filling in the advantages and disadvantages you discover for yourself will allow you to see quickly whether it makes sense for you.

Table 2.1 *List making as a tool for time management*

Advantages	Disadvantages
Takes away anxiety about forgetting to do things	
Having it on paper ensures that you don't forget	
Helps you to figure out what is important	
Provides an immediate progress report on what you have achieved	

You may have identified disadvantages such as: lists take too long to compile, they can seem over-fussy or nannyish, they may not be comprehensive, and what happens if you lose your list?

Despite these disadvantages, many people find list making essential, so here are some tips on effective list making.

Where to start

We suggest that you do this exercise at the end of the day, when you can start to plan ahead. Spend about five minutes considering what you'd like to achieve tomorrow. Compile a list of all the things you *have* to do tomorrow and all the things you *want* to do tomorrow.

Things I have to do tomorrow:

_____

_____

Things I want to do tomorrow:

_____

_____

Look at your lists and place a code letter A, B or C next to each one:

A next to things you must do or want to do tomorrow
B next to things you should do or would like to do by the end of the day, if you have time
C next to things you would like to do by the end of the day, but it won't matter if you don't.

Then look at all those categorized A and prioritize them into A1, A2 and so on, according to how important each item is. Estimate the amount of time your A list will take you to complete. If you have time, which item on the B list would be your first priority, and which your next? Plan your tomorrow so that you can complete your A list of priorities and some of the Bs if

there is time. Some days you may get to Cs. Review your achieve-
ment at the end of the day and then plan your next. Try out this
system every day for a week, making a new list for each day.

You may find that this way of planning doesn't exactly suit
you, so here are some tips to support the process. Bear these in
mind during this trial week.

◆ Make your new list at the end of each day, while you're still
  thinking about tasks to do for tomorrow. Lists help you
  switch off by removing the need to remember.
◆ Cross off items when they've been achieved. Build in small
  rewards for yourself for completing particular tasks.
◆ Ask yourself from time to time, 'Am I spending too much
  time on the B and C items?'.
◆ As something new occurs, add it to the list and letter code it
  according to its place in your priorities.
◆ Do keep the balance between what you must do and what
  you want to do. It's important to take care of some of your
  own needs.
◆ Ask yourself periodically, 'Am I doing what I want to do
  right now?'.
◆ Don't put off unpleasant jobs: they won't get any easier! Do
  them early so they don't hang over you.
◆ Link the completion of an A item that you 'must do' to
  addressing one that you 'want to do'.
◆ Transfer to tomorrow's list any uncompleted items from
  today's.
◆ If a C item remains on your list for more than three or four
  days, either upgrade it to A or B or cross it off and forget
  about it!
◆ Remember to build in 'thinking time' where necessary.
◆ Things like going shopping or writing reports often take
  longer than you think, so build in extra time (approximately
  20 per cent extra) if you can.
◆ Use short C jobs to act as energizers, or do one at the beginning of the day to get off to a successful start.

At the end of your trial week, ask yourself these questions:

How does a list help me?

_____

_____

How does it hinder me?

_____

_____

Did I forget anything?

_____

_____

Did I get more done? If so, why?

_____

_____

What did I do differently during the week when I made lists?

_____

_____

You will almost certainly want to adapt your list-making techniques to suit your personal needs. But, if you persist, you will
find list making and prioritizing to be a powerful tool in organizing your time.

As your time-management skills develop, you will become
aware that you have produced a number of lists and charts.

These are the basic tools with which to plan your time. As with any tools, it helps if you keep them all together, perhaps in a personal planner or organizer.

Most people are familiar with personal planners or organizers. They provide a convenient place to keep your daily lists, plus extra space to keep records and charts, and are essential for planning. However, you may prefer to use something larger and more roomy – a binder file or box, for instance. These are excellent for storing lots of information, but they are not very effective for detailed planning.

Planners need not be expensive; you can buy a notebook and customize it yourself. On the other hand, professionally produced planners are attractive and provide preprinted pages and charts. An advantage of many commercially available planners is their looseleaf binder system, which allows you to add and reposition pages as you like. A possible disadvantage of planners is their size; some of them are quite bulky. If this is an issue for you, choose a small, easily portable pocket calendar for essential daily information and a larger notebook for longer-term plans, charts and diagrams.

You may find that you use a box file for home organizing and a personal planner for work. Maybe a small pocket calendar would suffice if you were to put other information on an office wall chart. The important thing is to find something that suits you.

You can use the space below to make a list of items to keep in your personal planner.

What sort of things did you decide to keep in your planner? Was it just appointments or did you also list decisions that needed to be made? An advantage of listing decisions is that you can use your time more constructively because you won't be worrying for days about decisions that you need to make in the future.

Personal planner pages

Examples of two personal planner calendar pages follow. As you will see, the first is for a week and contains items relating to both home and work. The second is a daily one and covers mainly work. It might make sense for you to keep more than one planner, especially if you have a busy working day and a busy social life. If you are very involved in something like a political party or social club, you may want to keep a planner specifically for that.

Table 2.2 *Weekly calendar*

	Mon	Tue	Wed	Thu	Fri	Sat	Sun
Morning	*Prepare papers for afternoon meetings*	*Working at home*	*9–12 prepare report for board of directors meeting*		*Off to furniture shop in Wton with George*	*Go into town with children for shoes*	*Washing and ironing*
Afternoon	*12–2 meeting 2–4 meeting*	*Working at home*	*With Gill*	*1–4 attend ins. seminar*	*Lunch with George Travel back*		*Walk with children*
Evening	*Watch television*	*Make a meal for Christine and chat*	*Strip and varnish kitchen chairs*	*Late night shopping*	*Collapse and fall asleep in front of the television*	*Prepare some delicious food from new cookery book*	*Paint legs of kitchen chair*

Table 2.3 *Daily planner*

			Action
	06:00 AM		
	07:00 AM		Talk to
	08:00 AM	*Mike: review*	
Prepare presentation	09:00 AM	*Liz: notes for presentation*	
	10:00 AM	*Dennis: ideas for new programme*	
	11:00 AM		Telephone
Phone calls	12:00 PM	*Joanne Worth - job interview*	
Lunch	01:00 PM	*Moira re lunch*	
Presentation	02:00 PM	*Book tennis court*	
	03:00 PM		
Mike: review meeting	04:00 PM		Write to
Dictation	05:00 PM	*Minutes: SPR*	
	06:00 PM	*Meeting (see plans)*	
Tennis – Jerry	07:00 PM	*Norman Smith re bookings*	
	08:00 PM		Notes
	09:00 PM	*Pay bills*	
	10:00 PM	*Do expenses!*	
	11:00 PM	*Order stationery: pens, pads, 12 binders*	
	12:00 AM		

Gather together all the charts and lists that you have produced to plan your time. Sort them into those that go in the calendar section and those that go in the planner section. Below is an example of how you could do this.

Table 2.4 *Planner sorting*

Calendar	Planner
Priorities list for the week	Time investment record
Monthly calendar	Activity percentages chart
Weekly calendar	Satisfaction pies
Yearly calendar	Actual-time pies
	Use of time this week charts
	Motivational quotations or aphorisms

Your planner has everything you need to plan a more satisfying life. It is important to remember that it can only help you if you actually use it. Try to arrange a definite time each week for your planning activities.

Creating an efficient working environment

One objective of this chapter is to show you how an organized workspace, office or study can help you manage your time. Although we use the words 'office' and 'desk' in this section, the principles of creating a good working environment apply just as well to a home. Think about the difference between working in a clean, well-organized kitchen and a messy, chaotic one. Household tasks need as much organization as office work!

Imagine that you have a vital piece of work to do tomorrow. What would make you feel good about starting it? We believe that the following things are important:

◆ A *clear work space or desk* – this allows you to concentrate fully on the task.
◆ *The right tools for the job* – to avoid wasting time, make sure that you have the right equipment, books, stationery, supplies, files and data before you begin.
◆ *Peace and quiet (if possible)* – don't start an important job when you know that company is coming, the children are on their way home from school or the telephone will be particularly busy.
◆ A *comfortable work space* – you can't concentrate if you're conscious of your aching back or smarting eyes. Try to work in good light, sitting in a comfortable chair, at a work surface that is the right height.
◆ A *favourite picture on the wall or fresh flowers on your desk* – when you need to take a break, look at these and let your mind wander and relax.

Of course, you should try to be organized all the time, not just when you have an important job to do! Knowing exactly where things are can save hours.

The basis of a time-efficient approach to many jobs is a good filing system. This needn't be as technical as you might think; most people organize their household goods – for example, cleaning materials in one cabinet, food in another. Filing can mean anything from putting all the bills in an old shoe box or storing holiday photographs in a scrapbook to the more complex filing systems found in offices.

Filing systems

One excellent way of keeping track of information is to divide it into different sections. If you don't already use an efficient filing system at work, you could try the six categories that follow; at home, you will probably find that two or three of these categories will be enough. Use files or boxes to keep each section separate.

Table 2.5 *Filing sections*

File	Work that has been finished, but needs to be kept for reference
Do now	Items that need action today
Do soon	Jobs that must be done soon, but are not yet urgent
Read	Papers, magazines and reports
Pass on	Information that needs to go to another person with some comment or advice
Awaiting information	Jobs that need further information before anything can be done

If the system works, you will find that many jobs progress through most or all of these files. For example, an article that you must read comes in. You spot something that a colleague would be interested in and put it in the 'do soon' file. The next day you move it to the 'do now' file and you write a note, attach a copy of the article, and put the original article and a copy of the letter in the 'awaiting information' file. Your friend writes back thanking you, so the letter and article can be filed.

In and out trays
Trays can be very useful for keeping your papers all in one place. Make sure that any incoming letters, messages, or memos are put into the in tray straightaway. Look at the in tray regularly and, if necessary, transfer items to your filing system. When mail is due to be sent or given directly to another person, put these items in the out tray.

Noticeboards
Noticeboards are useful for reminding yourself about things at home and at work. They also let family and colleagues know what is happening or what needs to be done. The other benefit of noticeboards is that they can be as bright and colourful as you want. Being organized doesn't mean being dull!

Before we move on, don't forget other important places for putting papers – the wastebasket or recycling bin! Sometimes information is not worth keeping. Each time you receive a piece of paper, ask yourself, 'Do I need to keep this?'. If you don't, throw it away!

Now that you've worked through those ideas and tips, decide on any that you think you might use.

Is there anything you can do right now to improve the way you organize things?

Time cheaters and how to stop them

A 'time cheater' is something that robs us of a precious commodity – time to do the things we prefer. Time cheaters come in all shapes and sizes; they can be physical and mental; they can be created by ourselves or imposed on us by other people. What is important is to become aware of them; then we can learn to resist and deal with them.

Spend some time thinking about what stops or hinders you from doing the things that you want or need to do. Is there a neighbour or colleague who keeps you talking? Do you try to do too many things at the same time? Is your office or workroom disorganized? Make a note of any time cheaters that come to mind for you:

Time cheaters and time beaters

Our own time cheaters may have become so much a part of our world that they can be hard to discern, or perhaps there are too many to mention! Consider the list of time cheaters in Table 2.6 and, for each one, ask, 'Is this me?'. If it is one of your time cheaters, place a tick in the box and examine the possible solutions, or 'time beaters', suggested. A beater is a way of overcoming a cheater!

Now think of any changes that you will make to beat the time cheaters, and note them below.

Table 2.6 *Time cheaters*

Time cheater	Is this me?	Time beater
I spend too much time talking to people who won't go away		Learn to be more assertive. Say: 'I don't mean to be rude but I must get back to my work'
I get sidetracked easily and lack self-discipline		Make action plans and stick to them. Give yourself a reward (a treat) for good timekeeping
My colleagues/friends/children interrupt me all the time		Make clear to everyone when you don't want to be disturbed. Have regular 'quiet' periods that people know about and respect
I take on too much work		Learn to say 'no' politely but firmly. Being assertive means being polite but firm
Time runs out. I'm always rushed and late		Really think about what you have to do and how long it will take. Then add 20 per cent extra time to form a 'time cushion'
I get panicky and try to do everything at once		Prioritize! Spend five minutes quietly figuring out what jobs must be done and what can wait. Start at the top of your list and work through it steadily
I spend hours looking for papers and files		You need to get organized. Read through the section on filing systems again and start using different methods

Saving time

As discussed in Chapter 1, we can increase discretionary time by saving time spent on other activities, leaving us more time to do the things we want to do. Alternatively, we can increase our workload without increasing sold time, by performing work tasks more efficiently. Aside from knowing what we want to do now and doing it, there is no simple rule for saving time. Effective time use comes from examining our activities and finding ways of eliminating them or completing them more quickly.

Make a note overleaf of any ideas you have for saving time. It is not necessary to structure the ideas or evaluate them at this stage.

Now review your ideas and decide which ones you think will be most useful in helping you achieve more of that time in which you can choose what you do. Note these in your personal planner and build them into your planning activities.

The following are some time-saving techniques that others have found useful. Decide whether any of them might work for you.

◆ Use any waiting time constructively. Regard any waiting time not as a nuisance, but as a gift. If you have to wait for a train, plane or bus, or even for an appointment, use the time to plan something you have to work on, read a magazine article you need to read (you need to keep one with you for such occasions) or a chapter of a book that is on your 'must read' list.

◆ Combine activities. For example, have a work meeting over a pleasant lunch; hold a work conversation while strolling in the park; combine a meeting with a visit to a gym or a gentle jog. Make such work tasks more pleasant by associating them with something relaxing or fitness promoting.

◆ Have a place for everything and keep everything in its place. Being able to lay your hands on items when you need them, not having to wonder where something is, is not only time saving but also reduces frustration.

◆ For the same reason as above, maintain a good filing system. Having access to papers you need when you need them not only saves time but can enhance your reputation by creating an impression of good organization and preparedness.

◆ Remember that your first filing option is the rubbish bin. Ask yourself, 'Do I really need that piece of paper? What is the worst thing that could happen if I don't have it?'. Don't hoard what you don't need!

♦ Handle each piece of paper only once. Deal with it or file it the first time you pick it up.

♦ Always keep a notebook with you or near you. Don't lose an idea because you have nowhere to note it. Even keep a notepad by your bed. It's amazing how many problem-solving ideas come to us during the night and it can lose us sleep trying to remember them.

♦ Reinforce your time-saving efforts. Reward yourself with a treat, something you really enjoy, once you have completed a task.

♦ If flexitime is available or can be negotiated at work, use it to travel off-peak. Can you work more at home and be on-line to the office? Reducing travelling time can significantly increase productivity and quality of life.

♦ When it is possible, travelling by train rather than by car can allow you to complete a lot of reading and paperwork. It can be even more productive if you have access to a laptop computer.

♦ Delegate as much as you can. This is very developmental for others in your team, it increases your reputation as a manager (it shows you trust people and their abilities) and you get more of the things done that really need your talents and attention.

♦ Value your discretionary time as much as your paid time. Is the time you spend travelling to shop in a less expensive store always worth the money saved? Is it sometimes worth spending more to save time?

♦ If you can afford them, dishwashers, washing machines, microwaves, freezers and so on can all reduce maintenance time and boost your discretionary time. Might you consider employing domestic help?

♦ Constantly ask yourself, 'Is this the best use of my time right now?'.

You might be starting to feel as if all the spontaneity has been planned out of your life. But you will have more time to take things as they come if you plan the things you have to do. Time management enables us to be more focused, more clear and therefore more relaxed, with more time in which to relax.

Leisure time

Let's take a look at this open-ended resource that is discretionary time, the time available to choose what we want to do, the time available for leisure, and also at how we might choose to fill it and identify the many needs that it can fill.

First, let's consider the amount of discretionary time available to us. Is there any way of increasing it by cutting down on sold time and maintenance time? Alternatively, one way of dramatically altering the balance between sold time and discretionary time is to convert the discretionary activities into sold activities, much as musicians or professional athletes do. Even if we can't make a career choice out of a hobby, there will, as already discussed, be ways to increase our discretionary time by taking a more ordered, efficient approach to our sold and maintenance activities. Nevertheless, once we have reduced our sold time and maintenance time as much as is practical, we have expanded our discretionary time to its maximum within the constraints of our present circumstances.

The only way we can now increase our satisfaction from leisure is by making choices. The 'leisure pie' is now as big as it can be; you have to decide what ingredients will make it the best for you. It is useful, therefore, first to get a clear idea of what leisure means to you.

Jot down as many definitions of leisure as you can think of in three minutes.

Here are some that occurred to us:

◆ Leisure is attractive only when we choose it.
◆ Leisure time includes play time, enjoyed for its own sake.
◆ Leisure time is time at our disposal after paid work and

activities such as eating and sleeping (maintenance activities) have been completed.

◆ Leisure time is recreation time – time out from paid work to recharge our emotional, physical and intellectual batteries.

◆ Leisure and unemployment – we cannot ignore the concept of 'enforced leisure' and its attendant consequences.

◆ Leisure time is positive time. We can exercise powerful choice in its use and enjoy it at whatever level we choose.

◆ Our choice of leisure activity is entirely individual. Reasons for choosing one activity over another are subjective and complex.

What do you enjoy most?

If we have clear ideas about the types of leisure activities we enjoy, we are in a better position to make choices among different activities. The questionnaire in Table 2.7 is designed to help you to identify the features of the leisure activities you enjoy most. Read each statement carefully and decide how much you agree with it, circling the appropriate number against each, so that:

1 = Strongly disagree
2 = Disagree
3 = Not sure
4 = Agree
5 = Strongly agree

Draw a line under the first three groups. These three are your main leisure types. If you score highly in groups A, B, C, F, G, I, J, K, L or M, look at leisure activities to meet your emotional and social needs – how you feel and how you relate to others. If you score highly in groups E, H, K or L, seek activities that are geared to your physical needs – how your body feels. If you score highly in groups C, D, E, I or M, then concentrate on activities that satisfy your intellectual needs – activities that stimulate your mind.

Are you surprised by your leisure needs as identified by completing the leisure quotient questionnaire?

Table 2.7 *Leisure quotient questionnaire*

Interest group A – Being with people

1	2	3	4	5	I enjoy being in a crowd
1	2	3	4	5	I like talking to people
1	2	3	4	5	Who I'm with is more important than what I'm doing
1	2	3	4	5	I like joining clubs

Add up your score   Total =

Interest group B – Being with family

1	2	3	4	5	I like to plan family outings
1	2	3	4	5	I enjoy evenings when the family gets together to talk and relax
1	2	3	4	5	I get on with all generations in my family
1	2	3	4	5	I miss members of my family when we spend a long time apart

Add up your score   Total =

Interest group C – Being alone

1	2	3	4	5	I enjoy my own company
1	2	3	4	5	I like to be concentrating on something without stopping to talk
1	2	3	4	5	I enjoy having a room or space of my own
1	2	3	4	5	I like to rely on my own judgement

Add up your score   Total =

Interest group D – Using your brain

1	2	3	4	5	I enjoy time to think, plan and decide
1	2	3	4	5	I jump at an idea and like to follow it up for myself
1	2	3	4	5	I like reading and learning new facts
1	2	3	4	5	I enjoy discussing problems and issues

Add up your score   Total =

Interest group E – Making something

1	2	3	4	5	I like to see an end product for my efforts
1	2	3	4	5	I enjoy using my hands
1	2	3	4	5	I feel happy working with tools and machines
1	2	3	4	5	I like physical activity

Add up your score   Total =

Interest group F – Helping others

1	2	3	4	5	I like to feel useful
1	2	3	4	5	I like showing people how to solve problems
1	2	3	4	5	I enjoy giving some of my time to good causes
1	2	3	4	5	I think we're here to help other people feel better

Add up your score   Total =

Interest group G – Being different

1	2	3	4	5	I like to stand out in a crowd
1	2	3	4	5	I enjoy doing the opposite to what people expect
1	2	3	4	5	I like to make up my own mind
1	2	3	4	5	I like exploring new ways of doing things

Add up your score   Total =

Interest group H – Exercising

1	2	3	4	5	I like to be very fit
1	2	3	4	5	I enjoy physical activity
1	2	3	4	5	I like being outdoors
1	2	3	4	5	I like to meet difficult physical challenges

Add up your score   Total =

Interest group I – Being creative

1	2	3	4	5	I like to use my imagination
1	2	3	4	5	I like to express myself through art, crafts, music or writing
1	2	3	4	5	I like to daydream
1	2	3	4	5	I like being in an environment where people use their imaginations

Add up your score   Total =

Interest group J – Competing with others

1	2	3	4	5	I enjoy winning
1	2	3	4	5	I like to do things to the best of my ability
1	2	3	4	5	I like to find out if I can do things better than other people
1	2	3	4	5	Being second isn't good enough

Add up your score   Total =

Interest group K – Appreciating nature

1	2	3	4	5	I prefer the country to the city
1	2	3	4	5	I enjoy seeing beautiful scenery
1	2	3	4	5	I like to learn about nature from books and television programmes
1	2	3	4	5	I like animals and plants

Add up your score   Total =

Interest group L – Escaping from stress

1	2	3	4	5	I like to find ways to 'wind down' after work
1	2	3	4	5	I like things that take my attention away from problems
1	2	3	4	5	I like to take off spontaneously and do something unexpected
1	2	3	4	5	Relaxing is as important as working

Add up your score   Total =

Interest group M – Being entertained

1	2	3	4	5	I like being a member of an audience
1	2	3	4	5	I like looking out for events that I can go to
1	2	3	4	5	I like being diverted by a sports event, concert, play, film, TV show
1	2	3	4	5	I like talking about an event I've enjoyed

Add up your score   Total =

Add up your score for each interest group, then rank your groups in order, placing the interest group with the highest score first, and so on.

Group	Score
1	
2	
3	
4	
5	
6	
7	
8	
9	
10	
11	
12	
13	

Table 2.8 *Leisure activities table*

Interest group A – Being with people

Amusement parks	Dancing	Restaurants
Antique shows	Football	Shopping
Art class	Golf	Tennis
Bowling	Movies	Theatre
Camping	Museums	Zoos
Cards	Night school	
Clubs	Parks	

Interest group B – Being with family

Bicycling	Hiking	Reading
Board games	Holidays	Stamp collecting
Boating	Jigsaw puzzles	Table tennis
Camping	Model making	Television
Cooking	Museums	Zoos
Fishing	Neighbourhood restaurant	

Interest group C – Being alone

Bird watching	Painting	Swimming
Coin/stamp collecting	Photography	Television
Crossword puzzles	Reading	Woodworking
Jogging	Sewing	Writing
Meditation	Sightseeing	Yoga
Music	Hi-fi	

Interest group D – Using your brain

Archaeology	Flying	Night school
Art galleries	Genealogy	Reading
Astronomy	Inventing	Sailing
Book clubs	Lectures	Travel
Chess	Museums	Word puzzles

Interest group E – Making something

Baking	Nature collections	Sewing
Designing	Painting	Weaving
Gardening	Pottery	Wine making
Knitting	Restoring antiques	Woodworking
Leather craft	Scrapbooks	Writing
Model making	Sculpture	

Interest group F – Helping others

Babysitting	Environmentalism	Repairs
Charity sales	Giving a massage	Sponsored events
Driving	Listening	Voluntary work
Entertaining	Meals on Wheels	

Interest group G – Being different
Hang gliding	Rock climbing
Performance art	Sky diving

Interest group H – Exercising
Athletics/sports	Ice skating	Tennis
Bicycling	Jogging	Volleyball
Calisthenics/aerobics	Racquet sports	Weightlifting
Canoeing	Skiing	Yoga
Dancing	Soccer	
Horse riding	Swimming	

Interest group I – Being creative
Acting	Flower arranging	Pottery
Carving	Gardening	Sculpture
Choreography	Leather craft	Sketching
Composing	Model making	Weaving
Cooking/baking	Needlework	Writing
Decorating	Painting	
Directing	Photography	

Interest group J – Competing with others
Animal showing	Boxing	Golf
Archery	Cards	Racing
Baseball	Chess	Soccer
Basketball	Dance contests	Tennis
Board games	Exhibiting	Weightlifting
Bowling	Football	

Interest group K – Appreciating nature
Archaeology	Geology	Rock climbing
Astronomy	Hiking	Sailing
Beachcombing	Landscaping	Sketching
Camping	Nature programmes	Walking
Fishing	Parks	Zoos
Gardening	Riding	

Interest group L – Escaping from stress
Amusement parks	Parks	Television
Having a massage	Physical activity	Travel
Jogging	Radio	Visiting
Movies	Reading	Walking
Painting	Sunbathing	

Interest group M – Being entertained
Ballet	Movies	Hi-fi
Circus	Reading	Television
Concerts	Sightseeing	Theatre
Conversation	Spectator sports	

People in each of the three leisure types have leisure activities that suit them best. Take your three highest scoring groups and consider the activities suggested for each of these groups in the leisure activities table (Table 2.8).

Explore the activities listed in your three highest scoring groups, and use Table 2.9 to evaluate them by weighing the advantages and disadvantages of each one. This offers you the opportunity to consider new leisure activities that are suited to your leisure type, but that you might not have thought about before. Table 2.10 is an example of one person's chart.

Table 2.9 *Activity evaluation*

Leisure activity	Advantages	Disadvantages

Table 2.10 *Activity evaluation example*

Leisure activity	Advantages	Disadvantages
Archery	New skill Outdoor activity Meet new people Romantic Can rent equipment Exercise	Cost of equipment Travelling time Dangerous Never done it before
Card games	Win money Meet people Play anywhere	I always lose I gamble recklessly Boring Gets in the way of talking Don't like sitting still!

Review your chart and highlight the new activities for which the advantages outweigh the disadvantages. Include these new activities when planning your discretionary time. Consider carefully your stated disadvantages. Reactions such as 'boring' and 'take too much time' often conceal the real reasons for our reluctance – reasons we don't like to admit to ourselves. Asserting that something is boring often disguises the fact that we don't have the skills to do it successfully. Only by acknowledging that we don't have the skills can we be in a position to begin to acquire them.

Another way to expand your leisure choices is to look for events in your local newspaper and underline activities you have not done before but might like to try. You can also take advantage of the facilities of libraries and community centres in your area, as they usually have many different activities taking place. Consider setting yourself a target to do one new thing each week for the next four weeks. Incorporate these new activities into your planner.

Compose a list of 10 things you enjoy doing.

How can you start doing more of these things now?

You have identified your own leisure needs and explored new choices for your leisure. You have acquired the skills and techniques for evaluating these new leisure activities. Given that your discretionary time is limited, you will have to choose between your leisure activities, both old and new. As always, prioritizing activities is key to making the best of leisure time.

Personal review

Time management means organizing yourself in order to achieve what you want with your time. Its aim is not to fill up our lives with activity, but rather to assist us in identifying what we want from life and in planning how to go about getting it. Working through the material in this chapter has introduced you to using a number of techniques to achieve this. It is worthwhile to re-evaluate these techniques.

You are invited to read through the list of techniques and reflect on your experience of using them. Which have worked for you? Why did you find them successful? Which didn't suit you? Why do you think this is?

Time investment record:

Time diary and rank order activity sheets:

Satisfaction and actual-time pie comparisons:

Priorities for this week:

List making:

_____

_____

List prioritizing:

_____

_____

Using a diary:

_____

_____

Using a planner:

_____

_____

Creating an efficient working environment:

_____

_____

Time cheaters:

_____

_____

Time beaters:

_____

_____

We hope you have enjoyed working through the material so far and that you have achieved what you wanted from it.

Look back at your personal objectives. Has your thinking changed since then? If it has, record your new ideas about time.

_____

_____

This is an opportune time to review what you have gained and begin applying it. Make a note of what you have discovered about yourself and the way in which you manage your time. What techniques will you find helpful to improve your time management?

_____

_____

The goal is not to make a plan and stick to it, but to create a plan and constantly ask yourself the question, 'Is this working?'. If it isn't, it's time to revise the plan. Try to reserve some time each month to review how you are using your time.

PART II

SMART WORKING MEANS GETTING YOUR MESSAGE ACROSS - INTERPERSONAL COMMUNICATION

Have you ever wondered about, or even marvelled at, how air traffic is handled? It is amazing how aircraft from all over the world come and go at airports such as Heathrow with hardly a mishap. It is true that air traffic controllers, the people who 'handle' the aircraft, never touch them. All they ever do is communicate with the pilots. Nothing more, nothing less. Air traffic controllers provide information, give instructions, answer questions, clarify communications, calm anxious or confused pilots, take messages, solve a multitude of problems and co-ordinate the ever-changing work of pilots of all nationalities without ever seeing them face to face. It is done voice-to-voice, to coin a phrase! There is no body language, or clues from facial expressions; just verbal interaction on a two-way radio. And if you listen in to their communication, you hear only a calm, pleasant, non-threatening voice. There is no shouting, whining, cajoling, threatening or pouting. More often than not, they even say 'Please' and 'Thank you'. They manage purely by verbal communication.

Imagine what would happen if you were put in an isolated box where all you could do was talk by radio to your team or your colleagues. How well would you do? Can you even imagine how you would begin? One way would be to take another look at the air traffic controllers and see how they do it.

If you did, a few conditions would become obvious. First, they operate as part of an extraordinarily well-defined communications system where as little as possible is left to chance. The language is clear and precise; there is only one way to say, 'Cleared to land on runway 17'. 'Put her down on 17 or 45 as you please' won't do; nor will 'Land when you get around to it'. 'Cleared to land on runway 17' has only one meaning: land that thing now on runway 17.

A second aspect of the controller–pilot communication system is that the line of authority is very well defined. There is no question about who is in charge in an exchange between a pilot and a controller. It is the latter. There are rules to settle differences should they arise. For example, if you, as a pilot, predict that you will overshoot runway 17, then the solution is simple – ask permission from the controller to abort your landing and complete a very specific manoeuvre according to the controller's instructions that will put you in place to try another approach.

Could you duplicate such a communication system in your work environment? Probably not. Would you want to duplicate such a system? Probably not.

If you agree, note a couple of reasons why you would not choose to have such a strict, well-defined system in your work environment. What might the disadvantages be?

If your answer indicates that the goals of your work environment encourage differences of opinion, free exchanges and use of imagination, and that the risks of errors in communication in most work situations are not the matter of life and death they are in the illustration, then you get the point. Nevertheless, you may admit in private that it certainly would be nice if Jill asked clear questions, Bob spoke in complete sentences and Harry and Nell didn't jump to conclusions and become so emotional when there is a misunderstanding.

If you have observed interpersonal communication 'problems' in your work environment, what are they and how do you think they might be solved? Just jot down two or three suggestions concerning communication changes that might help.

Now go a step further and speculate about what it would take to have your suggestions accepted and implemented in your group or organization.

If there is a truth to be stated here, it is that there is always more to be said about anything. Whether it needs to be said, of course, is another matter.

Observe that, without saying so, we have been communicating about communication for the last few minutes. You are invited to continue discussing face-to-face communication in Chapters 3 and 4. As you continue, keep in mind the observations that you have just made about communication systems in general, and the problems and solutions in your work environment in particular.

3

STRAIGHT TALK

This chapter discusses communication skills that are basic competencies for effective managers at any level. It is probably true that, as with dancing and walking on your hands, some people seem to come by those skills naturally. Others need a little help and practice.

In either case, one of the important outcomes of managers studying these basic interpersonal communication skills is the language about language learned in the process. In other words, if one of your goals is to help employees communicate more effectively, it is important that you can communicate with them about basic communications. For example, can you write a definition for each of the following communication terms? Try it.

Sender:

_____

_____

Receiver:

_____

_____

Distortion:

_____

_____

Self-talk:

_____

_____

Tone:

_____

_____

Pitch:

It should be interesting to review your definitions after completing Chapter 3.

Let's explore what we mean by interpersonal communication. We will first look at the purpose of communication, then at the practical skills needed to communicate effectively, and offer you opportunities to identify and practise the skills you would like to develop. Our objectives in this section are, therefore, to:

◆ identify the part played in our lives by face-to-face communication
◆ identify factors that interfere with effective face-to-face communication
◆ identify skills that contribute to effective face-to-face communication
◆ identify speaking skills that contribute to good communication
◆ identify the part played by non-verbal factors in one-to-one communication
◆ identify skills needed to give and receive feedback
◆ identify skills of negotiation and managing conflict
◆ practise face-to-face communication skills.

What is interpersonal communication?

A great deal of our lives is taken up with communication. We are influenced in many ways by the communication systems we call the media – newspapers, radio and television. We also spend a considerable amount of time in contact with other people. Each of these contacts involves communication – talking, arguing, exchanging ideas, chatting, listening, giving information, voicing our opinions, our feelings and so on.

Most communication happens without individuals being very conscious of what is going on between them. If the communication is good we will probably benefit, but if it is not so good we may run into problems: we have all heard the phrases 'lack of communication' and 'communication breakdown'.

Let's concentrate on interpersonal communication – the communication that takes place between people who are talking face to face. This sort of communicating is something each of us begins to do normally from the time we are born. We learn to speak as we learn to walk, play and dress ourselves, so it's perhaps tempting to assume that our communication skills come to us as part of our natural development. Yet some people develop into very effective communicators, while others barely reach survival level.

Why are communication skills important? Without communication there would be no relationships, no organizations. Sharing ideas, giving opinions, finding out what we need to know, explaining what we want, resolving our differences with others and expressing our feelings are all examples of the kind of face-to-face communication that is essential if we are to relate to and work with other people.

Good managers know that the key to effective management lies in successfully managing people and relationships, not simply production figures or balance sheets. Good communication is the cornerstone of a successful enterprise. Experts have shown that in industry people spend more time communicating with other people than in any other activity, including production. When communication fails, production breaks down and quality and service are impaired.

What happens when two people talk to each other face to face? Look carefully at the conversation taking place in the cartoon in Figure 3.1.

We can begin to describe what is happening more clearly with a simple diagram (Figure 3.2).

In most conversations we continually move backwards and forwards between the roles of sender and receiver, rather like the ball in a game of tennis.

Figure 3.1

SENDER	RECEIVER	PURPOSE
the person who is speaking for some reason to the...	who is listening for the moment to find out the...	reason for the communication

Figure 3.2 *Communication flowchart*

What makes a good communicator? There are certain qualities that help us communicate effectively:

◆ *Respect* – making other people feel valued and important.
◆ *Honesty* – coming across as genuine, not being pretentious or playing games.
◆ *Empathy* – trying to see things from the other person's point of view as we share our ideas.

These qualities provide the foundation on which to build and develop the communication skills that we go on to explore.

What's it for?

Think about the amount of face-to-face communication that takes place every day in our lives. Use the chart in Table 3.1 to develop your own personal communication record for a typical day. Enter details of all your contacts with other people that involved communication, on a typical day in the last week. Yesterday will be freshest in your memory, but choose another day if that was not typical.

Table 3.1 *Communication record*

Communication record for .... (day)

People involved	Purpose	Results

Your notes might look something like this:

Table 3.2 *Communication record example*

Communication record for .... (day)

People involved	Purpose	Results
Me – daughter	To find out why she didn't get home by 10 pm	Agreed she'll ring me next time she's late
Me – boss	To agree to most convenient day to have off next week	Agreed to take Thursday off
Me – plumber	To arrange visit Thursday morning to fix sink pipe	Agreed to come at 9 am
Me – secretary	To rearrange 2 appointments scheduled for next Thursday	Secretary made arrangements
Me – client No. 1	To discuss contract	Contract agreed
Me – client No. 2	To go through queries about contract	Queries answered
Me – children	To tell them we'll go to Alton Towers on Thursday	Ecstatic screams
Me – ex-husband	To negotiate which of us has the kids this weekend	Fierce argument – usual problem

Without intruding, observe a range of face-to-face communications over one day. Use the chart in Table 3.3 to record some of these communications, their purpose and the results. You may find it interesting – and sometimes surprising – to check out with those involved what their experiences were of some of those exchanges, to note the differences between your perception of what went on and their own. There are likely to be different perceptions of any communication, as each of us is a unique individual and no two of us ever see the world and its events in quite the same way.

Table 3.3 *Observer's communication record*

Observer's communication record for .... (day)

People involved	Purpose	Results

Once you have observed some detailed examples of face-to-face communication, think about the general purpose of communicating. Why do people communicate? Write down at least four general reasons from the purpose columns of your lists.

People communicate for many different reasons:

◆ to inform
◆ to find out
◆ to learn
◆ to persuade
◆ to cooperate
◆ to amuse or entertain
◆ to negotiate
◆ to supervise or direct
◆ to help or support.

Each of us spends many hours of our day communicating with others. In total, several years of our lives will be spent on this activity. If we communicate well we are likely to be successful in many things we want to achieve. If we do not communicate well we could miss out on many opportunities. Particularly in management, clarity and quality of communication with those we manage are cornerstones of motivation and effectiveness.

Think about the possible results of good and poor communication. Jot down what you see as the benefits and potential pitfalls.

If we communicate well we will be able to:

_____

_____

If we communicate ineffectively it could mean:

_____

_____

Over the next week, observe people communicating in all kinds of context. Look for an example of really good communication and an example of less skilful communication. Reflect on what the senders and receivers were doing in each case. Jot down what you think made the difference.

An example of good communication:

_____

_____

Why I regard it as 'good':

_____

_____

An example of less skilful communication:

_____

_____

Why I judged this as less skilful:

_____

_____

_____

Good communication brings obvious benefits. We can influence others, learn more, get more of what we want, form better relationships, settle differences, help others and even make the world a better place! Poor communication is likely to cause difficulties. Relationships will be poor, learning will be harder, other people will find us confusing, we will be unable to achieve our ambitions, we will be unlikely to be able to help others, we will probably find life frustrating and unfulfilling. It follows that good communicators are likely to find life more satisfying and more rewarding because they are more able to shape events. In the next section, we look in more detail at the skills required.

Passing it on

Let us first identify factors that interfere with face-to-face communication.

Distortion

When we are listening to another person, even when we think we are concentrating, the message that we pick up is likely to be affected by a number of factors. If we pass the message on it may change significantly, as evidenced in the game Chinese Whispers. This change in the message is known as distortion.

Consider Figure 3.3. How we hear things and then report them to others can substantially erode or reshape an original message.

Figure 3.3

Think back over the last week. Can you think of an example in your own circumstances of communication that may have been distorted? Describe the situation, and suggest reasons why the message was distorted.

The situation:

_____

_____

The message may have been distorted because:

You may have recalled episodes where distortions in communications were caused by:

◆ the listener's own agenda, or resistance to what was being said
◆ the listener perhaps being impatient to put forward a point of view, with the result that he or she did not listen
◆ the listener perhaps simply 'switching off' because there were distractions
◆ a judgement that perhaps it was inappropriate to pass on parts of the message, and so on.

Distortion has many causes and is almost inevitable.

You may also have thought of an example of an interaction in which wires have been crossed: two people each thought they had a clear idea of what had been said, but both had quite different interpretations of a particular episode. This is not an unusual occurrence in patterns of communication that involve feelings. It is very easy to allow our own feelings to get in the way of hearing what another person is trying to say; and, of course, the other person may have similar interference operating at the same time. Added to this, it is not always easy to check out what has been said; the assumption is that the other person understands what we meant to say and the result is a scenario of many possible complications.

One of the factors that affects this sort of communication is our self-talk.

Shut your eyes and try not to think of anything in particular for 30 seconds or so; try to empty your mind. You will have found (unless you have been trained to make your mind blank) that your head is full of pictures, words, sounds, snatches of sentences and sensations. This babble goes on all the time. Our brain 'talks' to us constantly about the world around us; it filters this jumble of impressions and makes sense of it in our own terms. Most of the time we are unaware of our brain's activity but, without it, our thoughts would be just a ragbag of sights, sounds and sensations with no meaning.

We do not react instantly to situations. Our senses take everything in, then our brain picks out the things that are relevant for us in that situation and works out what we feel about it. As a result of this self-talk, we react.

The process of events is shown in Figure 3.4.

EVENT ————————▶ SELF-TALK ————————▶ REACTION

Figure 3.4 *Communication process*

Human beings think four times faster than they talk, so while we are listening a great many things are buzzing through our minds. What we are telling ourselves about the person who is speaking to us, about the matter they are talking about, about how we want to respond, will all affect how, how much and what we hear. If our relationship with the speaker is a negative one (we may have had differences with them in the past) we are likely to 'self-talk' ourselves into a challenging stance on anything new they might want to say. If we have expertise ourselves on the topic being discussed, our self-talk can lead us into premature questioning of what we are hearing rather than listening to what is being said. Other factors, such as shortage of time, can mean that we self-talk ourselves into a position of impatience and again our quality of listening can be impaired.

We can control our own self-talk and consequently cut out this kind of distortion. Once we are aware of any negative patterns in our self-talk, we can work on replacing them with positive, constructive thoughts. It helps to have some positive statements at the ready.

Can you think of any ways to counteract any negative self-talk you may experience while listening to particular individuals or particular topics? Ask yourself:

Who in the work environment do I find it most difficult to listen to objectively?

_____

_____

What am I telling myself while listening to that individual?

_____

_____

Which topics do I find it most difficult to listen to patiently?

_____

_____

What do I tell myself that distorts my listening to that topic?

_____

_____

What could I tell myself positively to improve my listening in each case?

_____

_____

Can you think of any other reasons for distortion? Jot down your thoughts.

_____

_____

Did your reasons include any of the following?

◆ Having to listen to a great deal of information can mean we pick up only part of it.
◆ If the subject bores us we do not listen as attentively as we do if we find the subject interesting.

◆ If what we listen to is too technical or full of unfamiliar jargon we can become frustrated.
◆ If we do not want to listen and be involved, or if we would rather be somewhere else, then we switch off.

You have begun to make a list of factors which will hinder communication – a list of things to avoid. Knowing what can go wrong is the first step to identifying the factors that will help communication. Before going on to the next section, spend some time observing people talking and listening to each other. Over the next three days, notice what people around you do that helps or hinders the messages that flow between them.

Getting it right

Let's consider now those factors that will help to make face-to-face communication more effective; that is, the skills of sending and receiving interpersonal messages.

As you watched people talking and listening to each other, what did you notice? Based on your observations, what helps or hinders the quality of communication?

_____

_____

You have already looked at some of the factors that can interfere with good communication. The following task builds on the work you did in the previous activities to enable you to produce some guidelines for good communication.

The sender

Watch one or two discussion programmes or interviews on television, or some communication interactions round the office. Concentrate on the role of the sender. This may be the interviewer or the person who is presenting his or her case. Focus on one aspect at a time – for example, things that help the sender get her or his message across. Then focus on those things that hinder sending, that mean that the sender is less effective in getting her or his message across. Turn your observations into some 'dos' and 'don'ts' of effective communication. List your tips below.

Dos (things that help sending):

_____

Don'ts (things that hinder sending):

_____

_____

Did your list of dos and don'ts include any of those on the checklist in Table 3.4? Tick the ones with which you agree.

Looking at the list of dos and don'ts for the sender, are there any that you would recognize as sometimes a part of your communication pattern? Make a note of one thing to watch out for and one thing that you know you do well.

I will watch out for:

_____

_____

I am good at:

_____

_____

Table 3.4 *Sender checklist*

Tick	Dos
	Be clear about what you want to say, focus and avoid distractions. If you are confused or unclear your listener is likely to be so as well.
	Look at the person you are speaking to. Eye contact is key to getting your point across. Failing to do so can suggest uncertainty, a lack of conviction or even evasion.
	Speak clearly. This seems obvious, but our natural style and pace of speaking may not suit every individual in every circumstance.
	Be in touch with the feelings of the person you are speaking to. Good communicators put themselves in their listeners' shoes and monitor how they are feeling about what they are hearing.
	Ensure that your words match your tone and body language. Mixed messages confuse and damage trust.
	Check that the other person has understood what you have said. Summarize from time to time, so you ensure that the listener is with you as your 'picture' unfolds.
	Vary the tone and pace at which you speak so that your voice is interesting to listent to. A monotone soon becomes monotonous!

Tick	Don'ts
	Don't complicate what you are saying with too much detail or difficult language. Remember that what you are saying may be new to the other person and they will be more in sympathy with what is conveyed clearly.
	Don't talk so much that the other person has no chance to comment or ask questions. Monologues prevent interaction and can cause the listener to 'switch off'.
	Don't be vague. Give concrete examples of what you mean.
	Don't put down, attack or ridicule the person to whom you are talking or their ideas.
	If you want them to hear and accept what you are saying, they will need to feel respected.
	Avoid ideas or examples that will irritate the other person. Irritants block listening.
	Look out for signs of confusion, resentment or disinterest. Be prepared to change tack.
	Avoid detached, remote messages. Speak with conviction, but avoid 'oversell'.

The receiver

Of course, listening skills are as vital as the skills of putting your point across. Listening is not the same as hearing. We can listen without hearing when we are mentally resisting what somebody wants to get across to us. Observe some interactions around the office and look for examples when somebody seems to be 'listening without hearing'.

Continue to observe examples of communication in your work setting. This time focus on the listeners (the receivers). Ask yourself what they do, or what they don't do, that helps and hinders the quality of the exchange. Note your observations.

Dos (what the receiver does that encourages quality communication):

_____

_____

Don'ts (what the receiver does that impairs the quality of communication):

_____

_____

Now compare your dos and don'ts with those in the checklist in Table 3.5. Tick the ones that you have also observed on other occasions.

Make a note of one or two things that you will particularly observe in your own communication style.

I will particularly:

_____

_____

Table 3.5 *Receiver checklist*

Tick	Dos
	Look at the person who is speaking to you. We can listen with our face turned away, but the signals will say 'disinterest'.
	Listen for the feelings behind the words. Showing that we are on the speaker's wavelength builds communication bridges.
	Look for points to agree with rather than to argue with. Hear the speaker out, avoid taking issue with points and arguing en route.
	Check that you have heard correctly by giving full attention, facing them, using nods and comments that show you are listening. Basic courtesy and respect for your speaker clears the communication channels.

Tick	Don'ts
	Avoid interruptions that break up the speaker's thought process and flow of communication.
	Avoid distractions, which again will break the flow.
	Don't let your previous experience of the person deflect your listening. This does not mean that you shouldn't take what you know of the speaker into consideration, but try not to prejudge what is being said – this time could be different!
	Don't let prejudices about particular topics get in the way of what is being said. Keep a look out for your pet irritants. Be especially careful when you know that a particular subject is a touchy one for you.
	Avoid any 'know-all' tendencies that might belittle or negate what is being said.
	Show respect for the speaker's point of view. Debate the point without 'having a go' at the speaker.
	Don't change the subject until closure is appropriate.
	Don't fidget or distract the speaker.

Are you more confident of your skills as a sender or as a receiver? People are often better at one role than the other. Think how often you have heard the comment, 'She's a good listener'. If you find that people often come to talk to you about their problems, the chances are that you are skilful at listening and receiving messages. If people often come to you for advice, or opinions, or ask you to speak to other people on their behalf, you are probably also skilful at sending messages. Think about your own communication skills.

My main skills at sending/receiving are:

_____

_____

I would like to develop these skills as a sender/receiver:

_____

_____

Three steps I will take to improve my skills as a sender/receiver in the future are:

_____

_____

Not what you say, but the way that you say it!

The objectives of this section are to explore the part played by tone and general use of the voice in one-to-one communication and to suggest ways of developing helpful techniques to improve these aspects.

The way you speak

How do you estimate your own ability to use your voice? Do you tend to speak too quietly, or too fast? Do you vary the tone and pitch of your voice to emphasize points and keep a topic lively?

A few words about accent. Most people speak with an accent of some sort, either regional or national, and this is now regarded as acceptable and even desirable. In years gone by it was not considered a good thing to have an accent and radio and television presenters had to speak 'the Queen's English' (that is, the way the Royal Family speak). That is no longer the case and 'the Queen's English' is regarded as just another accent. Indeed, some businesses which use call centres are locating them in parts of the country where local accents are widely regarded as friendly and trustworthy. As long as we speak clearly and are understood, we need not worry about a regional accent.

If you can get hold of a recording machine of any kind, record yourself having a conversation with someone, or simply say a few things into the machine and play it back. If we are not used to hearing ourselves on tape, this can be a shock. We can sound quite different from the way we think we do because we don't hear ourselves as others hear us.

Listen to your recording of yourself and use the checklist in Table 3.6 to assess how you think your voice comes across.

Table 3.6 *How do you speak?*

Tick	
	Do you pronouce each word distinctly?
	Do you speak too fast?
	…or too slowly to keep people's attention?
	Do you run all your words together?
	Do you sound sincere?
	Do you sound too loud?
	… or too soft?
	Does your voice sound shrill or squeaky?
	Does your voice sound monotonous?
	Does your tone convey how you feel?

How did you do? Unless you have been trained to use your voice properly, you will probably have found one or two things you would like to work on. Read through the following points to see what may strike a chord for you, now that you have heard yourself.

♦ *Speaking clearly.* Nervousness and habit are the culprits here. Our speech might be blurred as a result of our feeling tense and clenching our jaw as we speak. Tighten your jaw, with your mouth half closed, and say 'clear diction is an asset', moving your clenched jaw as little as possible. Now unclench it, relax it by moving it up and down a few times, and say the same sentence again, moving your relaxed mouth and jaw freely. Can you hear and feel the difference? When we relax and breathe evenly we are more likely to open our mouth and, therefore, to speak more clearly.

♦ *Speed.* The speed at which we talk is generally affected by what we are talking about and how we feel about it. If we are excited we quicken up; if we are bored we slow down. We can convey urgency and importance by speeding up, but if we then speak too quickly all the time the urgency will be lost – and so will the clarity. Over-slow speech is also difficult to listen to. We may be pronouncing every word perfectly, but pauses, hesitation or just too slow a delivery can frustrate the listener.

♦ *Tone.* Tone of voice is a key element in any communication. It can convey sincerity, enthusiasm, distaste, contempt, indeed all facets of human emotion; it can tell the listener what we think about them; it will tell the listener how we feel about what we are talking about and affect their judgement of it. We believe that words are important, but most of the 'message' will be carried in our tone. We can make the same word mean several things. Try saying the word 'good' and make it sound in turn bored, sarcastic, pleased, over-joyed, angry, surprised, sincere, hurried and anything else you can think of. The skill is aligning our tone of voice with our words to get across what we aim to convey. It is very easy to allow our voice to give away other feelings like tiredness, frustration or impatience, when those things are inappropriate to the situation or to the person we are talking to.

◆ *Volume*. Speaking too quietly to be properly audible can result from a lack of confidence. Volume control relies on good, deep, regular breathing, which often becomes quick and shallow when we are nervous. Take a few deep breaths, preferably in the open air, prior to speaking – before an interview or a difficult situation, for instance. Speak with your chin up and speak to the person furthest from you. Varying the volume of our voice, provided it is not too extreme, will add interest and emphasis to what we are saying, but take care not to sound too theatrical.

◆ *Pitch*. The pitch of our voice can also be affected by nervousness and tension. Our throat muscles and vocal cords tighten and the voice can become squeaky or shrill. Again, take a deep breath and, as you breathe slowly out, say a few short words such as, 'I'd like to make this point'. Your voice will automatically sound better, as it is physically impossible to breathe out and keep our muscles tight at the same time.

So we have begun to explore the art and skill of communication, which goes beyond the words we use. In the next chapter let's take our exploration further into the non-verbal dimension of interpersonal communication and then build on that by considering particular areas of such interactions in the work setting.

4

MORE THAN TALK

Non-verbal communication adds to the excitement and meaning of communication, but can also lead to the misery of misunderstanding and mistrust. Thus it is important for a manager to have competencies for dealing with more complex communication challenges. Helping employees understand their jobs and work through problems of misunderstanding are just two applications of the material.

It's not all talk

Let's now identify the part played by non-verbal factors in one-to-one communication. It is natural to believe that communication equals talking. It need not be so. The people in the cartoon in Figure 4.1 are communicating without words.

Figure 4.1

Non-verbal communication describes all those elements that convey messages between people other than in words. Some would suggest that in some circumstances up to 90 per cent of what is communicated between people is carried by factors other than words. We get non-verbal messages from sources such as eyes, mouths, faces, the way people sit, stand, move, where people stand or sit in relation to each other, how they hold and move their hands, arms, legs and so on.

Whether we are aware of it or not, we are picking up and giving out non-verbal signals more or less all the time. The words we use to communicate are important, but frequently not as important as non-verbal signals, which carry so much additional information that their impact can be significantly more powerful than what is being said.

The three faces in Figure 4.2 each show very different expressions. What do you believe they might mean?

Figure 4.2

We thought of bored, happy, sad. Even if those individuals were saying 'That's interesting', 'I'm really sad about that', 'Yes, I'm having a great time', we would be more likely to believe their expression than their words.

Whenever we communicate face to face with other people, we unconsciously notice their expressions and movements and, on the basis of that behaviour, form impressions about what is going on. Behaviour carries the most powerful messages. If we learn to read these clues consciously and skilfully, we can discover a good deal about other people, in addition to anything they might say.

Now consider some examples of the kind of behaviour that gives us non-verbal clues. In the right-hand column of Table 4.1 suggest what possible meanings there might be in each clue.

Table 4.1 *Non-verbal clues*

Clue	Possible meanings
A person nodding his head	
A person shaking his head slowly/quickly	
A person turning her face away	
A person facing you, but eyes down or looking away	
Staring eyes, glaring eyes	
A slight smile	
Lips tightly closed	
Jaw dropped open	
A deep breath	
A sigh	
A broad smile	
A soft voice	
A loud voice	
A shaky voice, hesitant	

Jot down your responses to the following questions.

How conscious are you of non-verbal elements in interactions in the work setting? How big a part do they play in communication at work?

What do you think is the most expressive part of the body? Which part of us says most?

What can we read from a person's eyes?

Would you agree with the thoughts below?

◆ A great deal will go on in terms of non-verbal communication in most work settings. Cooperation, teamworking, conflict, disagreement, reluctance, compliance, resentment and demotivation will all be visible in aspects other than words. A fairly frequent comment made about managers who displease staff is that 'they don't walk the talk'. They don't practise what they preach; they say one thing and do another. It is important to realize that we are always communicating whether or not we are speaking.

◆ Most people say most messages are carried in the face – the face is the 'mirror of the soul'. The head and face communicate an enormous range of non-verbal messages. Of course, the messages we pick up are not always accurate. We can sometimes attach the wrong meaning to the non-verbal

clues we get from other people. Assumptions can be erro-
neous and we may have to check our assumptions by asking
questions.
◆ Eye contact is very important. It can convey interest,
respect, disinterest and boredom. It enables each of us to signal to the other to start or stop talking. It is especially important in the listener. Unless the person we are speaking to
looks at us, we are likely to think they are not listening.

Think about other ways in which we communicate with each
other without words:

◆ through body position
◆ through clothes
◆ through a physical setting.

Body posture
Posture can tell us a good deal about a person's feelings. The way
they sit, stand, move and walk can signal whether they are
relaxed, happy, dejected, tense or angry. We use our hands and
arms unconsciously to give added meaning to what we say. We
use them to emphasize points and to demonstrate feelings.

Over the next few days, consider the way other people hold
and move their bodies (including hands, arms and legs) when
they are communicating. From time to time, reflect on your own
body positions and the messages they convey. For the moment,
think through the examples of body posture messages described
in Table 4.2. In the right-hand column make notes about the
message(s) that you think each conveys.

Messages in clothes
What can we tell about a person from the clothes they wear?
They are often the shapers of first impressions. As contact continues we will gather more information about a person or a situation and the impact of what somebody is wearing may recede.
But it is probably true that what we wear will be a statement
about ourselves and it is skilful to be aware of that and ensure
that our appearance says what we want it to about us.

Table 4.2 *Body posture*

Clue	Possible meanings
Slumping in a chair	
Sitting upright on the edge of a chair	
Sitting leaning towards somebody	
Sitting with arms folded, legs crossed	
Hands clenched tight	
Hands open, arms reaching towards somebody	
Pacing up and down	
Shrugging shoulders	
Wringing hands	
Fiddling with keys, pencils	
Sitting still, relaxed and looking at somebody	
Leaning back on chair with hands behind head	

What kind of clothes do you feel comfortable in?

_____

_____

Is there a dress code at work? What are 'the messages' in the way people dress for work?

_____

_____

Are there different expectations about appearance for different levels and functions? What are the messages in that?

Are there clothes that another person might wear to work that you would find offputting or irritating?

How far are clothes a reliable guide to what a person is really like?

Clothes are likely to have different meanings in different settings. You may, for example, feel comfortable in jeans; jeans are acceptable clothes for leisure time but in most work settings would be frowned on. The clothes we wear at home or at work are likely to reflect the 'uniform' of the social group to which we belong. We tend to look for and recognize this uniform in other people. We may take less notice of, or even dislike, someone who is obviously wearing a different 'uniform'. Some experts suggest that we are more likely to be successful at job interviews if we 'dress up' and wear the 'uniform' of someone in the tier above our present position.

Clothes may not be a reliable guide to what a person is actually like. They don't really tell us how punctual or efficient someone is, how caring they are or how much money they have. You may even feel that it is unfair or superficial to judge a person by the clothes they wear. But the evidence is that what we wear and how we wear it do matter. Clothes that are inappropriate for the circumstances will get in the way of what we want to communicate.

Physical setting

The way in which we arrange ourselves and our furniture in the space we occupy also conveys important non-verbal messages. Look at Figure 4.3.

Figure 4.3

What does the physical setting tell you about the relationship between the people in each situation?

_____

_____

Observe people standing around when they are in conversation. How directly do they face each other? Is there an ideal distance or position that makes talking easy? How much shifting about and movement is there? What can be read into any of this?

_____

_____

There are, of course, important cultural differences in the way people use physical space and organize their physical setting. In the UK, outside the home, there is generally little physical contact between people. Unless they are very friendly, a handshake is likely to be the only acceptable form of making contact. Being too far apart or too close makes conversation difficult. The most acceptable distance in white British culture is about two-and-a-half feet. If people stand or sit too close to each other they are likely to feel uncomfortable. Test this out by moving closer than you would normally to someone you are talking to. They will almost certainly move away.

Two people communicating around a table are likely to use the positions shown in Figure 4.4.

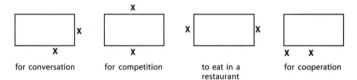

| for conversation | for competition | to eat in a restaurant | for cooperation |

Figure 4.4 *Positions*

Physical barriers between people, like desks and tables, are likely to suggest separation and distance in the relationship. Being behind a desk, sitting on a higher chair or standing over somebody can convey a position of power. Now think about how you can apply these observations in the way you use your own space.

If someone came into your room and you wanted to make them feel uncomfortable, how could you arrange yourself and the other person to do that?

If you wanted someone to feel comfortable and welcome, how could you arrange that?

If a stranger visited your home, what might he or she be able
to decide about you, just by looking around your living room?

From these activities, you will have reminded yourself that non-
verbal communication is a significant factor in person-to-person
communication. We will be sending signals about ourselves,
whether we are aware of it or not. How we dress, sit, stand and
walk will all tell other people about us, so it is important to be
aware of the messages we might want to give and of how to give
them. Equally, we will want to make sure that we are not giving
out one message with our words and another with our face and
body!

As we communicate, we are likely to be able to tell from the
other person's face how our message is being received; whether
our ideas, views and questions are being listened to, understood,
agreed with and so on. We can observe when we might need to
repeat or rephrase something, when it might be better to with-
draw and what effect our spoken words are having on the listener's feelings.

As a listener or receiver, we will need to be aware of using
non-verbal signals that show our interest – eye contact, nod-
ding, appropriate facial expressions, turning towards the speaker,
leaning forward if we are sitting down and so on. Our body is
always communicating. The key signals in talking and listening
are likely to be:

◆ facing the person
◆ keeping an open posture
◆ leaning towards the person
◆ maintaining good eye contact
◆ being relaxed.

Now consider how you will apply your awareness of non-verbal communication in your day-to-day contact with other people, and in your layout and use of your own workspace.

Three things I will work on to improve the way I communicate non-verbally:

Giving and receiving feedback

A good deal of people-to-people communication at work is in the form of feedback.

When people tell us how they feel about a job we have done, about the results of a project, the conduct of a meeting or a comment we have made, this is feedback. Feedback is a way of learning more about ourselves and the effect that our behaviour has on others. If feedback is constructive and is given skilfully, it increases self-awareness and encourages personal development. If feedback is destructive or given in an unskilled way, it simply leaves the person receiving it feeling bad, with no concrete goals to aim for. This does not mean to say that all constructive feedback must be positive. Negative feedback, given skilfully, can also be useful and important for our development and that of other people.

Recalling an occasion when you received feedback on something you did or said that you found positive and helpful, describe the situation and try to give reasons why you found it constructive.

As a manager you are likely to have to give feedback on regular occasions to members of your team on their performance or the results of a particular piece of work. If your own feelings about receiving feedback were positive, it is likely that the person giving it was skilful and used some of the following guidelines. See if you recognize any of them.

Ways of making feedback helpful and constructive – guidelines for giving feedback

1 *Be clear about your purpose. Feedback is a means of motivating and guiding somebody to better performance. It is more than just giving your opinion of somebody or getting 'something off your chest' and it is different from straightforward praise and criticism!*

2 *Work out what it is you want to get across to the person. It matters to get it right so prepare carefully, think ahead and collect any information or data you will need to support what you have to say.*

3 *Choose the time and place well. You need the person to be receptive to what you have to say, so do ensure that the situation is conducive to a quality exchange. The place needs to be free of distractions and free from the intrusion of third parties; the time needs to be one when you are both free to focus on and give full attention to the task.*

4 *Start with the positive. Your task is to keep the person listening to what you have to say. It is important to you, and to them, that they are receptive. Starting with a negative usually causes people to become defensive and to become reluctant listeners. A positive opening, the recognition of what they have done well, signals that you are not writing them off and are seeking to be constructive.*

5 *Focus on specific behaviour or results. The use of generalizations ('You have not done as well as expected recently' or even 'You have performed well overall') is usually unhelpful in as much as they can leave a person feeling good or bad without their actually understanding too much about the causes. Focusing on specifics ('The fact that your customer satisfaction rating was only 80 per cent disappointed me' or 'Your sales increase of 23 per cent really impressed me and the management team!') helps the person to be*

clear what it is they are being asked to avoid or repeat in the next phase.

6 Describe what happened, and what resulted, rather than being judgmental. Coming across as judge or critic is again likely to reduce the other person's readiness to listen and respond. ('Your being late for team meetings on three occasions annoyed me and others in the team' is likely to be more useful than 'You are unreliable and lack commitment!'.)

7 Focus on key areas. Attempting to cover too much can easily lose the other person and leave them confused. Concentrate on key successes and key areas for improvement and keep things clear and simple.

8 Ask for ideas and suggestions rather than simply making statements: 'How else could you have tackled that?'; 'In what other ways could I have helped?' Questions like these make the process a two-way dialogue, not simply a boss's monologue which most people hate. Involve people in their reviews or block their development!

9 Summarize or ask the other person to do so. Summaries significantly promote clarity of thought and progress in discussions. They also help both parties to be sure that they are on the same wavelength and have the same understanding of what has transpired and what is required.

10 Remember that feedback tells as much about you as it does about the receiver. The quality of the feedback we give, the areas we choose to focus on and our readiness to listen all communicate things about ourselves as managers. We need to be aware that our feedback provides a statement about ourselves that we need to be happy with.

11 Own the feedback. It is important that we take responsibility for the feedback we offer. Beginning the feedback with 'I' or 'In my opinion' is a way of avoiding the impression that you are voicing a universally agreed opinion.

12 Leave the recipient with a choice. Skilled feedback offers people information about themselves in a way that leaves them with a choice of whether to act or not.

13 Give the feedback as soon as you can after the event you want to comment on. Immediacy promotes relevance. Otherwise, the

event may have been superseded by something that makes your original feedback meaningless.

Feedback is essential in the interests of development and continuous improvement.

Reflect on one occasion when you gave feedback to a person recently. Was the situation at home, at work or somewhere else?

_____

_____

What was your relationship to the person?

_____

After reading through the guidelines above, do you feel that the feedback you gave was constructive?

_____

_____

Which points do you feel you could work on to improve your feedback skills in the future?

_____

_____

If we are on the receiving end of feedback, we can help ourselves by encouraging the giver to use some of the above skills. We can also help ourselves by observing the following guidelines.

Guidelines for receiving feedback

1 Listen to the feedback rather than immediately rejecting it or arguing with it. Feedback can be uncomfortable to receive, but you may be at a disadvantage if you do not hear what people think of your work or performance. However, remember that you are entitled to your opinion and you may choose to ignore feedback if you feel that it is irrelevant or inaccurate.

2 Be clear about what is being said. Make sure that you understand the feedback or you may not be able to use it fully. Avoid jumping to conclusions or immediately becoming defensive.

3 Check it out with others rather than relying on only one source. If you rely on only one source of feedback, then you may imagine that the individual's opinion is shared by everybody. You may find that other people view you differently and this can keep the feedback in proportion.

4 Ask for the feedback you want but don't get. You may have to ask for feedback if you do not come by it naturally. Sometimes the feedback you get may be restricted to one aspect of your behaviour or performance and you may have to request feedback that you would find useful but do not get.

5 Decide what you will do as a result of the feedback. You can use feedback to help in your own development. When you receive it, you can assess its value, the consequences of ignoring it or using it and then decide what to do as a result of it.

6 Finally, thank the person for giving the feedback. You might benefit from it and it may not have been easy for the person to give.

Could you work on one or two of the above suggestions to improve your own skills and improve the feedback you get? Are any of them particularly relevant to your situation or to your reaction when receiving feedback? Make a note of any aspects of them you intend to use.

The area I intend to work on when receiving feedback is:

Giving and receiving feedback are not easy to do, nor always enjoyable. These guidelines may make it easier and prevent differences in perception developing into a conflict situation.

The next section deals with the subject of conflict, a potential breakdown in communication and how to manage it.

Discussions and arguments – managing conflict

It is often difficult to tell the difference between a discussion and an argument. Sometimes it is to do with our perception: the person putting their case may see it as a discussion while the other person sees it as an argument. Sometimes a situation will turn into one involving conflict as one person loses control of the situation and the other responds accordingly.

This section introduces five negotiating skills for managing conflict in our daily lives. These are basic skills of communication and assertiveness. The exercising of any kind of skill is a deliberate process. Clear thinking is the first skill. It is the ability to stay cool, understand and observe the process, and see the path that any exchange might take.

This does not mean that, having completed this section of the book, you will be able to manage any conflict situation, nor that you will suddenly be capable of keeping calm in any circumstance! It just means that awareness is the prerequisite to avoiding runaway feelings and the irrational responses that are at the heart of conflict. It is also as well to recognize that, even if we are adept at using them, these skills may not work because:

◆ it takes two to resolve a conflict
◆ people may not respond to what is basically assertive behaviour with assertive behaviour themselves. Someone who chooses to respond passively or aggressively opts out of the problem-solving process and you can then be left on your own in seeking a solution.

Having a basic knowledge of conflict-management skills will, however, give you more of a chance more of the time and leave you feeling that you did your best.

How do you feel about conflict? Jot down all the words which describe how you feel about interpersonal conflict. Do it quickly, without thinking too deeply.

The way we feel about conflict has a direct bearing on the way we instinctively handle it. Do you keep your head when you are under pressure or under attack? Are you a sulker, an exploder or a negotiator? Do you simmer, blow or run away? It helps to know our own behaviour patterns, so that we can modify our reactions at difficult times in order to put our case better.

Jot down now any words that come to mind as you think of yourself in a contentious situation.

Now check this with someone who knows you well – a colleague or a member of your family. They may be able to add a few more words to your list!

What are the causes of conflict?

Problem solving in conflict situations first requires us to know what the nature of the 'difference' is. Conflicts can be differences of:

◆ *Interests*. A row between a customer and a member of staff, or between departments, may well be a conflict of interests – a difference between what each of them wants out of the transaction.

◆ *Understanding.* I might think you are being quiet because you are sulking, but actually it is because you have a lot on your mind. This can cause a conflict of understanding, because there is a difference between what you are experiencing and what I understand.

◆ *Values.* An argument about a particular course of action in business or corporate life can be the result of a conflict of values. Our values, things we believe in deeply (like loyalty, honesty, competition and so on), can give us different stances and priorities from others with differing value patterns.

◆ *Style.* Conflict caused by one person wanting to do a job slowly and methodically and the other person wanting to do it quickly and with flair is to do with style. We each have our own personality style and way of working and can be impatient or resentful of those who tackle things differently.

◆ *Opinion.* I think a particular sales campaign is well designed and imaginative and you think that it is boring and in dreadful taste. This is an example of a conflict of opinion.

Think of two conflict situations that you have either been directly involved in, or have observed. Note down the situation, and then assess what the conflict was about. Classify the conflict in the terms outlined above (interests, understanding, values, style or opinion).

Situation 1:

The cause:

Situation 2:

The cause:

_____

_____

The five skills of negotiation

Knowing the basis of any conflict increases our chances of solving it, but that knowledge plus some specific skills will give us an even greater chance. There are three basic ways of dealing with conflict:

◆ aggressively – fight it
◆ passively – duck it
◆ assertively – negotiate it.

Return to the words you used at the beginning of this section, concerning conflict and your behaviour in a conflict situation. Which of the ways listed above do you think is generally your style? 'Fighting' or 'ducking' are not regarded as conflict-solving skills, as they usually result in escalating matters or postponing a resolution. If your style of behaviour is 'negotiate', then you are likely already to have developed negotiating skills. Let's see whether you agree what those skills are. We believe that they are as follows.

1 Spot it!

If you don't spot a conflict situation early enough, it becomes harder to manage. Spotting conflict is not as easy as it sounds, however, partly because it is sometimes the outcome of a difference that may not seem serious at first. Secondly, a situation can escalate very quickly once some spark ignites it. Perhaps we have been too involved ourselves to notice when it started or, for those of us who tend towards aggression, perhaps we simply didn't want it to stop!

Write down under the headings below some of the verbal and non-verbal indicators that might signal conflict.

Verbal signals:

_____

_____

Non-verbal signals:

_____

_____

You might have identified verbal indicators such as insults, sarcasm, 'slow loader' emphasis, complaint, challenge, refusal, denial and shouting. Non-verbal indicators might include door slamming, glaring, sighing, laughing inappropriately, violence, going very quiet, growing restless and agitated, and leaving the room. You may have thought of many more things – there are all sorts of inventive ways that people will use to signal that they are at odds with someone else.

Once you have spotted the spark, the next thing to do is:

2 *Understand it*
Look back at the conflict situations that you listed earlier and use one of them to define what the problem is. There may be more than one cause of conflict in any situation. To be able to resolve it, we need to see clearly each person's point of view.

3 *Look for a win/win solution*
Being sensitive to conflict clues and understanding the antagonist's point of view is important, but choosing the appropriate way to resolve it is a crucial skill. You can decide on one of three strategies.

You can:

◆ *look for the win/win* – a solution that satisfies or even pleases both adversaries
◆ *settle for a win/lose solution,* whereby one party ends up feeling they have 'lost' and their opponent has emerged feeling victorious
◆ *do nothing* – sometimes this is appropriate, as the opposing parties may not be ready to settle their differences. However, it is as well to double check with yourself that you haven't just ducked the issue.

The ultimate aim of negotiation is to settle an argument leaving everybody feeling that they have won or, at least, leaving nobody feeling that they have lost out. Can you recall conflicts you have experienced where the outcomes have been:

Win/win? What was it about the result made you decide that it was this?

_____

Win/lose? What placed the result in this category?

_____

Do nothing? Why was this decision taken?

_____

Once you have decided on the strategy you will go for, you will need to:

4 Act at the right time

The key to this skill is to stand back long enough to answer three important questions. You need to ask yourself:

◆ Is resolving this important enough to me to make the effort it will need?
◆ Do I have the time it will take to reach a solution?
◆ Is this the right time to act?

Finding a win/win solution requires cool thinking, collaboration and calm, and an identification of what outcomes would be experienced as a 'win' by each party. The best time to act, of course, is before the conflict begins, which is why we need to develop the first skill of spotting it. However, once we are in the situation we will need to keep control of our own emotions to be able to think clearly. Trying to see the other person's point of view can sometimes keep our mind off our own emotions and give us time to ask the appropriate questions.

5 Check it out

If we can establish what is acceptable to either party, we are closer to checking out with both parties what each might concede to achieve the win/win. When making the offers, check out acceptability and feelings to ensure that there is no lingering resentment.

Use the questionnaire in Table 4.3 to check out and analyse the next conflict situation in which you find yourself. By doing this, you will be able to pinpoint the process and skills involved. Alternatively, review a conflict you have experienced in the past to draw the learning from that.

You have now been introduced to the skills of negotiation – spotting conflict, understanding it, looking for a win/win situation, acting at the right time and checking it out. Use the skills and review them.

For the moment, simply note what you will particularly work on in future situations of potential conflict.

_____

_____

Table 4.3 *Check it out questionnaire*

1	When was your conflict?
2	Who was it with?
3	What was it about? (Describe the argument briefly.)

4 Causes – was the conflict because of: Tick
   (a) interests: the difference between what you wanted and what he/she wanted?
   (b) understanding: the difference between what you understood and what he/she understood?
   (c) values: the difference between what's important to you and what's important to him/her?
   (d) style: the difference between the way you work and the way he/she works?
   (e) opinion: the difference between what you think and what he/she thinks?
   Tick the box and note down briefly the actual cause.

5 Style of response – how did you react? Did you: Tick
   (a) feel angry and show it?
   (b) feel angry but avoid showing it?
   (c) feel angry but stay cool to deal with the situation?
6 Is this your usual reaction to conflict?

7 Did this style of response leave you feeling good: Tick
   (a) about yourself?
   (b) about the other person?
8 Negotiating the conflict – when you spotted the conflict, which kind of result/outcome did you decide to work for?

9 Did you understand clearly what the other person's point of view was?

   If not, what did you do to find out?

   If you did nothing to find out, why not?

10 Did you: Tick
    (a) want to win the argument and beat the other person?
    (b) know that you would lose, so there was no point in trying?
    (c) look for a way where there were no losers?

11 Did you: Tick
    (a) jump in quickly with your response?
    (b) pause to think before speaking?
    (c) let too much time go by before making your response?
12 Did you feel good/bad at the end of the conflict?

    Did the other person feel good/bad at the finish? Describe what you think his/her feelings were.

13 Who won?   Tick
    (a) You
    (b) Him/her
    (c) Both of you
    (d) Neither of you

Applying the learning

The objective of this section is to plan to develop your face-to-face communication skills further. Enhancing your skills will require you to have an opportunity to practise the skills we have been considering. This section suggests activities that will focus on situations when you might do this. To practise the skills you will need to agree a practice exercise with another person, while some exercises are perhaps best done in a small group of about four to six people.

If you are using this book at work, you might ask your training officer to arrange some opportunities for group work. If you are studying at home, think about the opportunities you might be able to create in order to work on these activities with other people.

Options for practising communication skills

Option 1
Seeing how other people communicate can help us improve our own skills. While sitting in a meeting, use the checklist in Table 4.4 to observe people communicating. Observe the skills they are demonstrating and tick off the ones that you see used.

Active learning – practising the skills
You can use the checklist in various other ways. For example:

◆ Watch a TV programme where people are involved in conversation or discussion. A chat show or question-and-answer format such as *Question Time* is probably best. Observe the senders and receivers and tick off the skills that you see being used.
◆ Agree a session with two other people. Each of you prepares a topic to talk on for five minutes. Each takes it in turn to be the sender (talking about the topic), the receiver (listening carefully to what the other person has to say) and the observer (using the checklist to watch and listen to the skills of the sender and receiver). Topics to talk about could be 'A

Table 4.4 *Practising communication skills – option 1*

Tick	Sender
	Seemed well prepared in what to say
	Spoke clearly
	Varied voice
	Presented one idea at a time clearly and avoided complication
	Made good eye contact with those he/she was speaking to
	Gave examples to increase clarity, avoided vagueness
	Paused to give people time for questions
	Used summaries to help keep others in the picture
	Treated listeners with respect, seemed friendly
	Verbal message consistent with non-verbal

Tick	Receiver
	Maintained eye contact with the speaker
	Faced the person, seemed relaxed and open
	Didn't interrupt
	Asked relevant questions to increase understanding
	Showed active interest
	Recognized other people's feelings
	Asked for clarification to increase understanding
	Was not critical, impatient or bored
	Showed concentration, sat or stood still, did not fidget
	Spoke clearly
	Did not 'take over' the exchange
	Summarized to check understanding

job I would really like', 'If I won the lottery', 'The best and worst things about where I live' or 'Violence and vandalism and what could be done about them'.

Another version may be useful if you spend a lot of time giving instructions or coaching other people. Each take turns as sender, receiver and observer as above, but instead of choosing a topic, each sender has to give very careful instructions on how to carry out a particular task – for example, how to use a laptop computer, use the Internet, prepare a presentation for management or plan a holiday.

If you prefer, choose a task at work or at home about which you often need to give instructions. Take about 10 minutes at the end of the exercise to give each other constructive feedback on what you have observed.

Option 2

This is an activity for three or four people. Each spends three or four minutes preparing to give their views on an opinion about which there is disagreement within the group – for example, 'Capital punishment should be brought back', 'Women's liberation is a good thing', 'Religion is out of date', 'Welfare dependency should be ended' and so on.

Let the first person speak to the rest of the group for about three minutes. The second person then summarizes the first person's views and briefly replies, giving their own views on the subject. The second person then speaks for three minutes, giving their point of view on a different topic. The third person then summarizes, replies and so on.

When the last person has spoken, the first person should summarize what they have said and reply, giving their views.

After doing this, discuss the questions below as a group and make notes.

How easy is it to listen accurately to what another person is saying? What makes it easy or difficult?

How easy is it to listen when you have things you want to say? What are the consequences of not listening?

Is it helpful to hear a summary of points you have made? If so, why?

How is communication in a group more difficult than between two people?

In your discussion you may be reminded of some of the things mentioned earlier about distortion. It is easy to be distracted from listening accurately if you have other things on your mind or are bursting to say something yourself. Summarizing is a helpful way of focusing accurately on what the sender is communicating. It gives the sender feedback about what has come across and whether the message has been understood; and it helps the receiver check that they are picking up the message accurately.

Option 3

This option offers an opportunity to think about an area that you find difficult to discuss with a particular person. It is an activity for a group of four to six people.

Working as a group, each thinks of at least one example of something you find difficult to talk about to someone. In Table 4.5 are some examples to prompt you. Add examples from your group.

Now as a group spend about 20 minutes discussing the examples you have chosen, using these questions to help you:

◆ Why is this topic difficult?
◆ What are the communication challenges when a topic is difficult?
◆ Is it difficult for everybody?
◆ What would be the anxieties of the sender and receiver?
◆ What particular skills does it help to focus on when the topic is difficult?

Now that you have reflected on and practised these ideas on interpersonal communication, here is a summary of the process

Table 4.5 *Practising communication skills – option 3*

It is difficult to talk about...	To...
a lack of quality support	your manager
a pay rise	your boss
wanting promotion	your boss
things that you are worried about or afraid of	someone who expects you to be strong
wanting to break off a relationship	your partner, boyfriend or girlfriend
frustrations or difficulties in your job	your boss or other colleagues
Your own examples:	

we have been considering that illustrates the model of face-to-face communication with what we have been exploring (Figure 4.5).

Action plan

Now that you have completed this self-study material on face-to-face communication, look back over the original objectives, including those that you may have set yourself. Have you achieved them? Now that you have worked through a number of tasks to help you increase your skills at communicating, how will you apply them? Use the following headings to help you draw up an action plan for yourself.

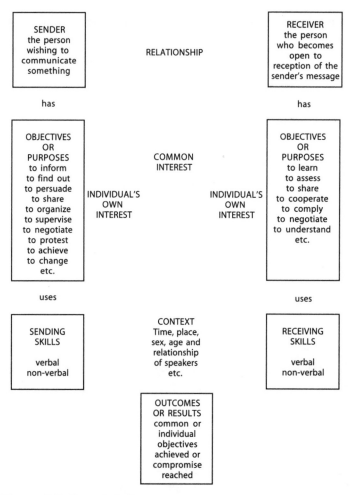

Figure 4.5 *A model of communication*

Two things I already do well when I communicate with other people:

_____

_____

Two things I particularly want to work on:

_____

_____

Two things I can do to improve my effectiveness as a sender:

_____

_____

Two things I can do to improve my effectiveness as a receiver:

_____

_____

Part III

Group Communication and Meetings

Let's consider now that particular area of business life and managers' activities – the successful planning and conduct of meetings.

Meetings, well planned and well run, are a great contributor to a positive work climate and productive communication. The effective manager will be alert to the need to prepare well for meetings, keep them on target, see that everyone has an opportunity to speak, encourage people to share their ideas, monitor group dynamics, ensure that the physical conditions support the meeting, keep working groups on task, keep track of the progress of subgroups and decide when it is appropriate to deviate from an agenda.

Some of these functions may come naturally to us, others may not. The good news is that there are many concepts and behaviours we can learn that will make the fit more comfortable and thus productive. Some of these will be considered in the material that follows.

5

MAKING MEETINGS WORK

Whether they are formal or informal, meetings are an integral part of any organization or group of people working together. People must talk, exchange ideas and information and co-ordinate their efforts. Unfortunately, meetings have a bad name in some organizations and are seen by many as a waste of time. As one cynic said, 'A meeting is a group of people who singly can do nothing and collectively decide that nothing can be done'.

This was once a common experience, but is becoming less so as organizations in both the private and public sectors become more task oriented, more dynamic and more conscious of the need for quality processes. Additionally, companies have fewer of the unwieldy and lengthy processes that the word 'meeting' once conjured up. Team meetings and project meetings currently tend to be as short and focused as possible and as small as possible. This material addresses the elements of conducting effective meetings.

What can go wrong?

It is probably true to say that we are all experts on meetings. In our working lives we have probably spent hundreds, even thousands, of hours attending meetings. In most organizations, however, meetings are not the most popular form of activity. In many cases, people would rather be involved in any other aspect of work than attend meetings. In short, meetings have had a bad press.

Let us reflect for a moment on some possible reasons for this poor reputation that meetings have. Think about the meetings that you have experienced in your work situation recently. There will no doubt be memories of meetings that went well, but perhaps many more memories of meetings that were frustrating, boring, fruitless or simply disappointing. If you were asked to think about the learning that might be drawn from such ineffective meetings what might that learning reveal?

Jot down some of the reasons for believing that meetings might frequently be ineffective.

Compare your recollections with the experiences of many other people who have answered that same question. Here are the reasons others have given on why meetings go wrong:

◆ They are not planned.
◆ They are too planned – everything seems 'sewn up'; there is no flexibility.
◆ Some people dominate the meetings; there's no real sharing of ideas.
◆ It isn't known what everyone thinks, because not everyone speaks.
◆ There's too much silence because it's too risky for people to talk.
◆ The necessary people aren't there.
◆ People interrupt each other and don't listen.
◆ Some people clearly don't want to be there.
◆ People play politics; they bring with them agendas from other times and other places.
◆ The meeting is too big and disorganized.
◆ There doesn't seem to be a definite purpose or clear agenda.
◆ Things are not well prepared; materials needed aren't ready.
◆ The meeting is organized at the wrong time – people are tired and can't concentrate.
◆ The meeting is structured to suit a few people – there is no

real discussion of topics that are important to many.
◆ The chair allows people to take too much 'air time' and doesn't stick to the agenda.
◆ There are strong differences of opinion and these are 'fudged' over.
◆ There isn't a proper decision-making procedure.
◆ People are aggressive towards others when they air their points of view.
◆ Some people seem unwilling to compromise.
◆ Some people are awkward and disruptive.
◆ The room for the meeting is too hot, stuffy, noisy, uncomfortable and so on.
◆ No proper records are kept of what has been decided.
◆ The meeting seems to drag on forever.
◆ There is never any follow up; the meeting is all talk and nothing ever happens as a result of it.

The list could have been longer, but we can see that in many organizations meetings take up a lot of time, create a great deal of frustration, even resentment, and are counterproductive.

How would you rate the meetings you hold or have to attend? Generally well run and effective, fairly well run and effective or not so well run or effective?

_____

_____

Why is that?

_____

_____

For many, the rating is 'not so well run'. So why have meetings? If you had to make a case for the value of meetings, what would you say were their potential benefits that make them so significant?

A well-run meeting:

♦ allows the involvement of whole teams in decision making and planning
♦ allows face-to-face communication and thus greater understanding
♦ allows the airing of feelings and therefore a more comprehensive working through of issues
♦ creates more involvement, and therefore more motivation, than paper-based or electronic communications
♦ means 'two plus two equals five' – a way of saying that the combined talents of people are likely to produce more than individuals acting separately.

Is a meeting really necessary?

This is a question that must be answered before you decide to go ahead with preparations for any meeting. Always ask yourself whether there are alternatives. These might be memos, phone calls, one-to-one discussions with the main decision maker, stand-up conferences in hallways or talking through an administrative problem over coffee. Before you hold your next meeting, read through the criteria in Table 5.1 to review whether a meeting is necessary.

The suggestions put forward in this table may not be suitable for a number of reasons particular to your own organization. It is as well to be aware of the shortcomings of your internal communication systems and to take these into account.

Table 5.2 contains a list of possible advantages and disadvantages of three suggested methods of communication – meetings, phone calls and memos. Add any other points as they occur to you.

Table 5.1 *Checklist – alternatives to meetings*

Are there more than five people who must all have the same information?	Memo
Does more than one person have to contribute to the body of information?	Meeting
Are there only a few points to communicate to a few people?	Phone calls
Are there only a few points to communicate to many people, with no need for discussion?	Memo
Is it important that everyone fully understands the information?	Meeting/phone calls (depending on numbers)
Is speed an important factor?	Meeting/phone calls (depending on numbers)
Does any decision require endorsement from a group of people? (For instance, if they are to act on it.)	Meeting
Does the reason merit the time and effort involved in a meeting?	Meeting
Is it important to promote teamwork?	Meeting

It is true that in the electronic age there is less need for work teams or groups to physically gather together in order to communicate and plan. However, in terms of real teamworking and teambuilding, the well-run, face-to-face meeting will probably always offer more than impersonal e-mails or even video conferencing. The key term is, of course, 'well-run'!

Planning effective meetings

It is interesting to study that list of the reasons for meetings 'going wrong'. It is a list that is full of learning and clues about what it takes to make meetings go well. Analysing that list, we can see that there are categories of issues. There are problems to do with:

◆ purpose and agenda
◆ time and timing
◆ the meeting place

Table 5.2 *Advantages and disadvantages of meetings*

Advantages	Disadvantages
Meetings	
Best way to give substantial or important information to larger groups	Can be time consuming
You can be sure that participants have received all the information	Takes time to arrange and gather all the participants
They can ask questions if they don't understand	Some people may not be able to attend at short notice
Best way to reach a decision that needs group action/approval	
Promotes teamwork	
Add your own	Add your own
Memos	
Quick to write yourself and copy, or to have typed and distributed	People do not always grasp the important of a memo and may not read it properly
All the information is recorded, everyone will have all the points	It may take time for them to receive it
Add your own	Add your own
Phone calls	
You can be sure that the information has been received and understood	Takes too much time, you can get sidetracked on to other matters
You can find out immediately if there are any problems	You may not be able to reach the people immediately and waste time trying
Add your own	Add your own

- chairing or facilitation
- people
- decisions
- action.

The problems that are there for all to see are also the keys to the successes locked in the same list. These problems lead us to a formula for planning effective meetings. Let's look at this in more detail.

Purpose and agenda

The essential starting point is for those who set up meetings to be sure that there is a clear purpose to them. Naturally, busy people are going to respond very negatively to being distracted from their other priorities in order to be present at an event that seems to be aimless. There needs to be clarity about what the meeting is for, whether it be decision making, information giving, consultation or planning. These purposes can of course be combined, but this needs to be clear ahead of shaping the agenda. We need to make sure that the purposes are clear to all and relevant, as well as achievable in the time allowed.

Agendas therefore contain those items compiled in pursuit of the purpose. Usually they will be compiled by those convening the meeting, but ideally they need also to be open to the members of the group attending, otherwise it will be difficult to create involvement. Those attending may offer agenda items ahead of the meeting or be able to add to the agenda at the meeting itself. We should be wary, however, of allowing a mass of late suggestions which can overwhelm the prepared agenda. Agendas and supporting papers need to be distributed well ahead of the meeting itself to allow for preparation. It will be helpful if the agenda makes clear:

- the purpose (objectives)
- starting and finishing times
- the venue
- which items are for information, which for discussion and which for decision making.

Time and timing

People attending meetings usually have to slot the event into their already crowded schedules. They need, therefore, to be able to rely on the starting and finishing times being strictly adhered to. They need to be confident that the meeting will be well organized and managed, enabling them to plan other work around it. Obviously, predicting the length of the meeting requires a fairly accurate estimate of the time each agenda item will take. An alternative approach is to state, for example, that there will be a two-hour meeting, prioritize the agenda items and deal with as many as possible in that time, leaving those remaining to be dealt with at a subsequent meeting.

It also pays dividends to think carefully about when in the working week to hold the meeting. Meetings late on a Friday afternoon, after a hectic week's work, are likely to be attended by people not at their best in terms of energy and creativity. In general, people are more likely to enjoy higher levels of energy in the morning than in the afternoon and, likewise, earlier rather than later in the week. Holding a series of meetings together on one day can be tempting, especially in organizations in which people spend a lot of time away from the office. Be wary, however, of 'meeting fatigue', which can adversely affect the later meetings.

How do the meetings you run or attend measure up in reality? How well would you rate them in terms of the following?

Are agendas well prepared and accessible to all those attending?

_____

_____

Is time well managed, with the stated starting and ending times being observed?

_____

_____

Are meetings held at the more 'creative' times of the day or week?

What do you believe would need to happen to make your meetings even more effective in terms of agenda and timing?

The meeting place

People work best, feel more valued and will perceive that a meeting is better organized if attention is paid to ensuring that the venue for the meeting is as attractive, comfortable and purposeful as it can be. The person responsible for convening the meeting needs to:

◆ give clear directions to the venue
◆ choose a comfortable, light, airy room, which is neither too hot nor too cold, with fresh air to keep people alert
◆ arrange a warm welcome, with refreshments if required
◆ arrange the room so that people are comfortable and can talk to each other
◆ set out just enough chairs, with no gaps separating those attending
◆ have flipcharts to keep the agenda visible and to record decisions and action planned.

Chairing, or facilitation, and people

A great deal of responsibility for the effectiveness of meetings rests, of course, with the person who chairs the event. The person in this leadership role needs to be very conscious of managing the meeting at two levels – the agenda and timing, and the people involved.

This requires skills comparable to those of a tightrope walker. Just as a tightrope walker has to maintain a very fine balance to succeed, so the chair of a meeting has to balance the business of the meeting with the participation of those attending and their satisfaction with the process and results.

It is as crucial to give attention to the people in a meeting as it is to give attention to the agenda. Unless participants go away feeling they have been listened to, that their attendance and contributions have been appreciated and that the meeting has been well organized and managed, they may not have the motivation required for future meetings or for the follow-up action for which they may be responsible. They will also expect the agenda to be relevant to them and well managed, with positive results emerging. They don't want ruthless, officious chairing that rigidly sticks to the agenda at any cost, but neither do they want a laid back, *laissez faire*, aimless kind of meeting. They want the chair to maintain the 'tightrope' balance; that is, to show appreciation, give them attention and get the business done as well!

The task of the chair can be described thus:

To facilitate completion of the agenda in the allocated time while allowing the balanced participation of those attending, so that they feel satisfied with the conduct of the meeting.

This suggests that an effective chair will combine 'people' skills with 'agenda' skills. Later on, we shall return to consider this pivotal role in more detail.

Decision making

Many items will involve decision making. It is important to be clear which agenda items need decisions and which do not – there may be points simply for information or discussion. For each item consider:

◆ whether a decision is necessary. If it is, be clear about the process – how will decisions be made?
◆ whether decisions will be made by consensus, by majority

voting, or by individuals after hearing opinions in the meeting. If majority voting is used, give particular attention to the minority, ensuring that they do not feel excluded afterwards .

◆ whether the responsibility for implementing decisions is clear. Is the whole group bound by the decisions?

◆ whether the timescale for making decisions and implementing the action is clear

◆ whether there is a need, at the end of the meeting, to clarify what decisions have been made and what tasks people are responsible for.

Occasionally, conflict may occur in the decision-making process. In that case, it is important that the chair:

◆ listens very carefully to what is, or is not, being said and how that is being expressed

◆ avoids taking sides but gets those with differing opinions to clarify the issues for the chair and for each other

◆ ensures that the discussion is focused on the present and on what progress might be made, rather than on personalities or past events

◆ prevents repetition by continually asking for options for a solution

◆ asks those who are not party to the difference of opinion for their suggested solutions

◆ seeks a win/win outcome – that is, looks for the common ground, for what can be agreed; asks those in dispute what they find acceptable about the others' case and what compromise they could be satisfied with.

If conflict emerges, we need, perhaps above all else, to stay calm and pursue solutions, telling ourselves and others that differences are a natural part of team dynamics. Indeed, differences can be celebrated. If teams work positively through difficulties they can become stronger and develop even more effective teamworking. Differences create energy and the possibility of creative solutions.

Action

Meetings are intended to make a difference; if they don't, there is no point in having them. Action for change has to emerge from all the talking. In chairing a meeting it is important to ensure that:

◆ action plans are made identifying what needs to happen next
◆ plans are recorded and those responsible for action are clearly identified
◆ there is a clear timetable for completing the action
◆ a progress report on the action taken is incorporated into the agenda of the next meeting.

How would you rate your current meetings in terms of:

the quality of the meeting place?

_____

_____
the involvement of those attending?

_____

_____
the quality of decision making?

_____

_____
action planning?

_____

_____

What would it take to improve the quality of your meetings in any of these areas?

Here is a checklist you can use to plan or review your meetings:

1 Notice of the meeting time and place is distributed in advance to all participants.
2 The agenda is prepared and circulated before the meeting.
3 All participants have an opportunity to contribute to the agenda.
4 Meeting facilities are checked for availability and suitability, and materials, such as pens and flipchart paper, or a whiteboard, are on hand if necessary.
5 Care is taken to ensure that there are no interruptions.
6 The meeting begins and ends on time.
7 The use of time is managed well throughout the meeting.
8 Everyone has an opportunity to speak.
9 Participants listen to each other.
10 No one dominates the discussions.
11 The items are summarized periodically.
12 The meeting ends with a full summary.
13 Minutes of the meetings, or action sheets, are distributed to each participant following the meeting.
14 Participants can be depended on to carry out any action agreed during the meeting.

If, on reviewing your meetings, it is normally possible to tick 12 or more of the statements on the checklist, that indicates that you are attending quality meetings. Less than eight ticks suggests that work is required to improve the quality of the meetings you attend.

Some more on the chair, or facilitator

As we have discussed, the chair or facilitator, is responsible for:

◆ seeing that the meeting achieves its objectives as efficiently as possible and within the time allocated
◆ balancing the participation of attendees
◆ clarifying or interpreting where necessary
◆ managing the agenda and the time
◆ ensuring that decisions are made by the group where necessary
◆ arranging for an accurate record of the meeting to be kept
◆ remaining impartial and acting for the members
◆ completing the agenda in such a way that those attending are happy with the process.

Let's now consider this key role in more detail. As we have also seen, the leadership skills required might be analysed in terms of 'agenda skills' and 'people skills'. They could also be analysed in terms of skills needed 'before, during and after' a meeting. Combining those categories of skills gives us a matrix covering the role of the chair (Table 5.3).

Consider that matrix of skills and reflect on your own chairing of meetings.

How many of the skills identified would you say you regularly demonstrate? Are there any you would particularly like to work on?

Table 5.4 is a checklist for evaluating your performance in this role, which will help you to identify your own strengths and those areas on which it would be valuable to work as part of your

Table 5.3 *Chair's skills matrix*

	The agenda	The people
Before the meeting	Prepare agenda while allowing those attending to offer items Communicate the objectives, venue, start and finishing time, giving plenty of notice Ensure all supporting papers are available	Ensure all those, and only those, who need to be there will be there Give those attending plenty of notice and the chance to offer items for the agenda
During the meeting	Start on time. Make clear the finishing time Make clear the order in which items will be dealt with Keep agenda visible to all. Tick off items dealt with to show progress and work still to do Keep visible minutes, e.g. decisions made and actions planned, on a flipchart Work through agenda, being flexible when key items need more time, but maintain momentum Summarize on completion of each item, then move on Manage the time. Keep the group in the picture about time remaining Summarize at the end – what has been achieved, what the next steps are Fix the date of the next meeting	Allow introductions if necessary Work for the balanced participation of everybody Encourage contributions. Manage those who take too much 'air time' and draw in those who are offering least Link the comments of one with points made by others to build flow and cohesion Explore differences of opinion by encouraging these to be talked through. Avoid taking sides but look for common ground Listen well and show appreciation of ideas and views offered Encourage the links between discussion and action by asking: 'What can we do about that?' Thank people for attending. Ask them if there are ways in which future meetings can be improved
After the meeting	Ensure actions planned and decisions made are followed up Distribute minutes/ record of the meeting Ask: 'What can I learn from how that meeting went?' 'Will I chair the next one differently? If so, how?' Prepare for the next meeting using the learning from this one	Consult people to check that they are progessing things that are their responsibility, support them as necessary Be open to ideas for the next agenda and for improving the style of meetings

Table 5.4 *Chair's evaluation*

How do you rate as a meeting chair?

Place a tick beside any question to which you can definitely answer 'yes'

	Tick
1 Did you convene the necessary people?	
2 Did the meeting have clear objectives?	
3 Did you start and finish the meeting on time?	
4 Were you as impartial as you could be?	
5 Did you keep the discussions on track?	
6 Had you gauged the timing for each item correctly?	
7 Did you encourage everyone to participate?	
8 Did you summarize fairly after each item?	
9 Did you help to resolve conflict while allowing participants to express their points of view?	
10 Did you make sure that action plans were developed and followed up afterwards?	

continuous development. Reflecting on a meeting that you have led recently, use the checklist as a general evaluation. Alternatively, wait until you have chaired your next meeting and evaluate yourself at that point.

However many ticks you have on this checklist, it can be useful to use it to review every meeting you chair, asking yourself, 'What did I do well in chairing that meeting?' and\ 'What will I focus on particularly when chairing my next meeting?'

Now consider each item in the checklist in more detail.

Inviting only those who need to be there
The smaller a meeting is, the more effective it generally is, especially if it is to be a decision-making or problem-solving meeting. If you invite only the people who are going to contribute, then they are likely to be motivated and committed to its

success. People to whom the agenda and purpose are less relevant are likely to be frustrated. Some people may need to be present for part of the business. They can attend at a certain time for their item only and leave afterwards.

 Does this have any application to your current meetings?

Clear objectives

A well-defined agenda goes a long way to delivering a meeting's objectives. Before you plan your agenda it is important to decide first what kind of meeting you are planning – information giving, consultation, decision making, problem solving. If it is a mixed agenda then mark the items as 'For Information', 'Decisions Needed' and so on. It is sometimes better to separate the different tasks. You may choose to have two meetings separated by a break and ask only the relevant few to attend the decision-making second half.

 Does this have any application to your current meetings?

Starting on time

Always start on time, even if not everybody is present. This shows those who have been punctual and sets the standard. Latecomers can be given a quick update when they arrive. Space can be left for them near the door so they can join the meeting with minimum disruption.

 Does this have any application to your current meetings?

Being impartial

Although there will be times when you, as chair, must contribute to discussions by giving your views, your primary role is one of facilitator. Literally, this means 'easing the path' for those present. You have to draw people out, elicit their opinions, link their comments and listen to every view, while always keeping the discussion relevant and focused. You must be a model of objective and open-minded behaviour and a seeker of common ground and ways forward. This will set the tone of the meeting.

There may also be times when you have to make a particular decision but need information and the opinions of others to do so. The requirement is always to be clear with everybody about the status of the discussion and the process in hand. You must be careful, in cases like this, to let everyone have their say whether it supports your own position or not.

Does this have any application to your current meetings?

_____

_____

Keeping people to the point

Keep people aware of the visible agenda and the current item being considered. Tick or cross out completed items. If discussion wanders, bring people firmly but politely back to the point. When linking individual contributions, tactful guidance is sometimes needed. Here is a list of useful ways to bring the discussion back to the point:

◆ Can we finish dealing with one point before starting on another?
◆ Several issues have been raised by X, let's take this one first.
◆ I think that point will be more relevant later, let's leave it until then and go back to...
◆ The relevance of that point to our objective is...
◆ How do you see that last point influencing what we are discussing?

♦ We've covered a number of points. Which one do you think is most important bearing in mind that our objective is…?

♦ Is this issue relevant to the matter in hand?

Occasional summaries can also steer the group or an individual back to the track if that has been lost. The task is to refocus the discussion without showing impatience or criticizing any individual. For this reason, giving some support to the person (that is, appreciating their contribution in some way as well as trying to keep future contributions to the point) will help strike a balance: 'You've said several interesting things there. The one that seems very important to me is… Has anyone else anything to say on this?'

Does this have any application to your current meetings?

_____

_____

Managing meeting time and monitoring each item

A well-thought-out agenda, with adequate time allocated to each item, is invaluable as a beginning. Unless more important matters emerge, calmly but fairly keep the discussions within the time limits. If you have to extend one item, make the group aware of the knock-on effects. When planning the agenda, be sure to allow enough time for each item and add a few minutes to each of your estimates as a cushion. If you have allowed too much time, then you have extra time for some other issue if you need it. Alternatively, nobody will mind if the meeting is shorter than expected. They will see it as an example of your efficiency.

Does this have any application to your current meetings?

_____

_____

Encouraging members to participate (and discouraging others!)

As chair, your task is to make the group work to maximum effectiveness with maximum participation from all members. There will always be those who will dominate the discussion and those who will say less. It is important for group or team cohesiveness that everyone has a chance to contribute.

It may be necessary to curtail the contributions of some to get air time for the less voluble. Going around the table, saying it matters to have everybody's views, is one way. Showing appreciation for the more effusive contributions, but saying 'We must hear from others', is another: 'So, Sara, the point you're making is helpful. What do you think, James?' Or you could be more specific in your intervention: 'Sara, if you can summarize your point then we can hear from... James, I believe you have had experience in this field. Is there anything we have overlooked?'

When using questions to stimulate discussion be sure to:

◆ ask open questions that provoke thought and reflection rather than merely 'yes' or 'no'
◆ keep the questions simple
◆ keep the focus on the topic in hand.

Does this have any application to your current meetings?

_____

_____

Periodic summarizing

Summaries are useful in many ways. They allow you and others to check understandings of what has been said or agreed and they are a means of drawing a line under one part of the agenda before moving on to the next. Summarizing also provides a way of keeping people to the point without appearing to 'put down' particular individuals.

Does this have any application to your current meetings?

_____

_____

Follow up

In the period after the meeting, it is essential in order to maintain motivation that you follow up and check out that any action promised has been carried out. Make sure that everyone receives a copy of the minutes or action sheet. After that, either agree a report-back at the next meeting or make support or 'check-out' phone calls to the relevant people at appropriate times.

Does this have any application to your current meetings?

_____

_____

Objectives and action plans

Reflect on this section and the learning for you. Collect together all the thoughts you have gathered on your own performance. From this, set yourself one or two clear objectives from each section.

Objectives

To improve the effectiveness of my meetings I will...

_____

_____

Build on your objectives and convert them into action plans.

Action plan

To achieve my objectives, I will…

_____

_____

How will you know when you have achieved your objectives?

I will review my progress on (date three months ahead)

_____

_____

and on (date six months ahead)

_____

_____

Enter these dates in your diary.

6

Some Further Thoughts – Making Sense of Group Behaviour

The purpose of this chapter is to gain a better understanding of principles and techniques that contribute to understanding and managing group behaviour and help you apply them. To achieve this purpose, you will need to read the material, complete the 'reader interactions' and follow up by doing the application exercises. It is helpful to read about and discuss group procedures, but ultimately group leadership competencies develop from applying what you have learned in real groups and reviewing feedback.

Groups are dynamic, or are usually intended to be. You have undoubtedly been a member of highly active groups as well as those that seem bogged down. There are a number of ways in which to understand group dynamics. One of these is the dual perspective of group business (its tasks) and group process (its methods). We will use the business/process frame of reference as a way of assisting you to improve communications in the groups in which you participate. As a manager, in most instances your function is that of group leader, but in others it will be as regular participant. In other words, as a manager you frequently have the responsibility of leading staff during meetings and, as a member of your management group, you have the responsibility of being a productive group member.

Content vs process

When we read the agenda of a group's meeting, we learn about the meeting's concerns. The agenda items are what is meant by the business of a group's meeting. If we understand the business (the topics or agenda) of a group's meeting, we have some idea of what it wants to accomplish, by when and, often, who is responsible for the various tasks involved. If you come late to a meeting and whisper to your neighbout 'What's going on?', the chances are that the answer will be in terms of content – the topics the group is discussing or the plans and decisions it is trying to make; that is, the business part of the meeting.

If, at the same meeting, we sit back and observe, we might discover that the agenda items have taken a back seat to what is actually going on (process). The observations that stand out most are: Bill trying to make political points with Susan, the chairperson; Harry cracking jokes aimed at distracting the group's attention from the agenda issues; Clyde chatting up Betty for a date after work; Barrie reading his mail and thus sending a message to everyone about how unimportant he thinks they and the meeting are; Neil pecking away at his laptop computer, because that's what he's really interested in; Martha talking quietly on her cellphone. In other words, we would be observing the dynamics of the group's process.

In this example, the group process seems to be going in as many directions as it has members, few of which are related to the stated agenda or purpose of the meeting. Group business (agenda) and process (way of working together) need to be compatible and mutually supportive. The key to this happening is a group leader (a chair) with adequate group skills who can assist the group in achieving its agenda goals. The process by which this is done should add pleasure to group meetings and contribute to developing group strength and cohesiveness. When business and process seem to be on separate tracks, the situation can soon develop into what is known as group chaos.

As noted, business and process are both important to group success. A group that tends to stick strictly to the agenda may complete it, but fail to implement its decisions once the meeting is over because it has not worked cohesively or been on the same wavelength. This is probably because the group has not developed as an entity of its own. Thus those people participating in the dull process feel no membership or commitment to the group. How could they? There is no group in the lasting sense of the term.

In contrast, a group that develops a wonderfully enjoyable process, full of humour and good spirits, may have a great time during its meeting, but never get around to dealing with the content of its agenda.

How does your group experience match these comments?

Business/process review

Describe a meeting you have attended recently in which the business (agenda) was clearly not supported by the group process (how the group worked, or did not work, together).

Now describe a meeting in which the business was supported by the group process.

Reflect on these two meetings. What made the difference? Note the conditions, people and events that help account for the differences between the two meetings.

The explanations that most people provide in this exercise are more often concerned with group process than the business of the meeting. What is the crux of your explanations? You can take the exercise a step further.

Describe an action that might have been taken before or during the first meeting you noted to keep the process from going astray. What could the chair, or somebody else, have done to create group cohesion and smooth the way it worked?

Any actions you may think of would usually be referred to as 'interventions', in that someone intervenes in the process and attempts to make it more supportive of the purpose of the meeting. As you have probably observed, however, a well-intended intervention can have the opposite effect.

The reasons for failed interventions fall into several categories. These include poor timing, unclear communication, negative connotations, inappropriate emotion, inaccurate perception of what is happening, that they are made by an unpopular person, and many other miscalculations and errors in behaviour. As we move through this section, several methods for helping ensure that interventions are effective will be discussed. Nevertheless, group intervention remains a complex and separate topic and there are no easy answers.

The more you practise business/process observations, the more skilful you are likely to become in managing groups. One suggestion for honing your process perception skills is to take a few minutes after each meeting to think about what took place during the meeting with regard to its agenda and process. Ask yourself what you might do in the future in a similar situation to make effective interventions, to help the group work more coherently and smoothly. Another suggestion is to work with a colleague to compare your notes and findings about group dynamics in the meetings you attend together.

Group dynamics

How does a manager get a grasp of what is happening in a group? Usually it is helpful to break down the processes of group dynamics into smaller components and try to understand them piece by piece. In the language of group dynamics, this is referred to as process observation. The objective of process observation is to answer the following three questions:

1   What is going on the group?
2   What is needed to make the group function more effectively?
3   How can the processes be changed to add the missing component and make the group function more effectively?

This section responds to all three of these questions, with particular emphasis on the first two and clear implications for question 3.

There are several procedures to aid clarification of what is taking place in the group. These include:

◆ tracking communication patterns – who talks to whom and in what way?
◆ identifying group member roles – who is contributing what to the group?
◆ analysing problem-solving styles
◆ clarifying decision-making methods
◆ assessing the group climate (the feeling and tone of the meeting)
◆ assessing situational and environmental variables (group size, physical facilities, room comfort).

In this section we will focus on understanding group processes by tracking and studying communication patterns and identifying group member roles and how they interact. These two process areas are relatively easy to understand. Once they have been understood, you can use them as a manager to assist groups to function more effectively.

Tracking communication patterns

Observing communication patterns is a good place to start. It is relatively easy and as a manager you can obtain a significant amount of information that will be useful in understanding how your group functions. Not the least of the outcomes of tracking communications is information about how you yourself are functioning in the group. Ideally, you would have a group member, who is not active in the meeting, acting solely as a process observer. As this is rarely possible, the next best approach is to tape or video a given meeting, playing it back to identify communication patterns.

The easiest record to track is 'who talks?' – using a 'Who Talks?' form to collect information. Blank copies of all the communication tracking forms can be found at the end of this chapter. An example of a completed 'Who Talks?' form follows in Table 6.1. Each member is listed in the Group Member column. A mark is made in the Contributions column each time someone speaks without pause or interruption, regardless of the length of the contribution. The figures for the Total and Percent columns are calculated when the session is over.

Table 6.1 is an example of a tally from a 30-minute discussion between six people.

Table 6.1 *Who talks?*

Group member	Contributions	Total	Percent
A	///////////	11	20
B	//	2	4
C	/////////////////	17	33
D	////////	8	14
E	///////	7	12
F	/////////	9	17
	Total	54	100

From looking at this record of the number of individual 'contributions', we can say that C seemed to dominate the meeting. But is that really true? It is possible that person C is a 'yes' person and the only contribution made may have been to say 'That's good' after every other group member said something. Secretly, the staff call C the 'cheerleader' and your record verifies that C has the greatest frequency of contributions.

In order to gain a better understanding of communication patterns, modify the procedure to record only contributions of 15 seconds or longer. Again, make a tally mark for each contribution and then make further marks for each 15 seconds that a single communication continues.

The results of such a tally for the same group of six are illustrated in Table 6.2, 'Who Talks? How Long?' Marks grouped together indicate a contribution longer than 15 seconds, so that /// indicates a single 45-second contribution.

Table 6.2 *Who talks? How long?*

Group member	Contributions	Total	Percent
A	/// / / // /// /	6	32
B		0	0
C	/ //	2	11
D	// / /	3	16
E	/	1	5
F	/ //// // / ///// / //	7	37
	Total	19	100

How would you now interpret the process that took place in that meeting?

This record identifies the long-winded member! Even though person A talks six times and person F talks seven times, F takes significantly more air time. You've probably known some colleagues like this.

A third communication pattern to observe is interruptions. You can use the 'Who Interrupts Whom?' grid. This is easy to use. The name of each group member is written across the top of the form and again along the left-hand side. There is an example in Table 6.3 of a 10-minute meeting of five people.

Table 6.3 *Who interrupts whom?*

Name	Alan	Barbara	Carl	Debbie	Ed	Total
Alan interrupts					/	1
Barbara interrupts	/		/		/	3
Carl interrupts						0
Debbie interrupts	/					1
Ed interrupts				/		1
Total	2	0	1	1	2	

What do interruptions mean? They can mean several things. Long-winded people tend to be interrupted. Higher-status people tend to interrupt lower-status people. Watch out, Ms/Mr Manager – perhaps you do this! Few people interrupt the boss.

In the segment above, Barbara interrupted three times but was never interrupted herself. Possible explanations might be that she is the leader of the group or that the only way she knows of entering a conversation is by interrupting. If you take the time to observe them, interruptions tell a story about a group.

A fourth communication pattern to observe is 'Who Talks? After Whom?' This record can identify people who support or reject one another. Again, use a grid with the names of the group members along the top and left side. Note who each group member speaks after, tally as before, but this time also note if the contribution made was + (supportive); – (rejecting); or ^ (neutral). There is an example in Table 6.4 of a 'Who Talks? After Whom' grid for the same five-member group as the previous example.

Table 6.4 *Who talks? After whom?*

Name	Alan	Barbara	Carl	Debbie	Ed
Alan talks after		^	+	^+++^^^	^
Barbara talks after	^		+		^^^
Carl talks after	+^	^^		+	^^
Debbie talks after	^^+^	^^^	^+		+^
Ed talks after	^^	^	^^	-^^	
Total	7^3+	7^	3^3+	4+1-6^	7^1+

Notice that in this example no one talks in a supportive way after Barbara. Perhaps Barbara's ideas are not seen as that good by other group members. Notice also that Alan and Debbie talk after each other and usually in a supportive way. Possibly they are friends or, more specifically, are in agreement with the ideas being presented.

We have presented four ways to track communication patterns:

◆ Who talks?
◆ Who talks? How long?
◆ Who interrupts whom?
◆ Who talks? After whom?

What might be the main value in tracking communication patterns?

If you mentioned something to the effect that the record is specific, factual and is descriptive of the actual behaviour, you are on the right track. Monitoring communication patterns provides you as a manager with an objective basis for analysing and promoting more effective group behaviour. Instead of offering a vague observation that an employee interrupts often, or talks more than their share of the time, you can present actual data and base the discussion on it.

Here are ways to extend the communication tracking process. Use the four blank forms at the end of the chapter to record these four types of communication patterns for your group. This can be done in various ways. For example:

◆ Track the communication yourself while the meeting is in progress, focusing on just one of the communication patterns for a 10-minute period. Repeat the procedure, paying attention to other kinds of communication pattern.
◆ Tape record the group without tracking the communication, then listen to the tape and complete the forms, focusing on one of the communication patterns for a 10-minute period. Continue listening to the recording, this time focusing on other communication patterns.
◆ Appoint someone not involved in the meeting to record the types of communication pattern.

The use of any of these methods would, of course, need to be agreed with those attending the meeting. If people understand that you are working to make meetings more effective and to improve your own chairing skills, they are likely to agree to the tracking taking place. After you have studied the results from the tracking, provide feedback, at an appropriate time, to individuals and the group regarding the communication patterns observed.

Observing communication patterns is a way to begin clarifying what is going on in a given meeting at a given time. Remember that one set of data is usually not sufficient information for making final judgements about why a group is performing effectively or ineffectively, but it can provide meaningful insights into both effective and ineffective patterns of communication that may not otherwise be apparent.

Member roles

For this analysis we will focus on three types of group behaviour:

◆ *'Agenda/task' behaviours* – those behaviours that primarily help the group achieve its task and complete the agenda.
◆ *'Process/maintenance' behaviours* – those behaviours that develop and maintain the group.
◆ *'Self-oriented' behaviours* – those behaviours that meet the personal needs of an individual member but do not assist the group to achieve its tasks or maintain itself. Sometimes these are called anti-group behaviours or perhaps, to use a better phrase, less helpful behaviours.

For a group to be functioning well it needs both agenda/task and process/maintenance behaviours in a balance appropriate for its needs. One might think that a group only needs agenda/task behaviours. However, if it uses only these behaviours it might get the job done, but the members may not like one another well enough to enable it to complete another job. If, on the other hand, a group uses only process/maintenance behaviours, members may enjoy interacting with one another to such an extent that they avoid getting the job done, or avoid dealing with and resolving conflicts and disagreements. The result may be that they are unable to reach their objectives.

Self-oriented behaviours develop for a variety of reasons. They are a means by which people express disagreement with group methods or even tasks. Some self-oriented behaviour may even be an individual's means of expressing resentment over being included in the group. In more extreme cases, people who consistently display self-oriented behaviour detrimental to a group's performance may simply lack group interaction skills. Whatever the cause, persistent self-oriented behaviour should be recognized, confronted and resolved. This is probably best achieved with one-to-one feedback, outside the meeting, for the individual producing the difficulty. The slight unpleasantness involved in intervening is usually a much smaller price to pay than allowing the disruption based on self-oriented behaviour to grow into a significant group problem.

If you are able to, recall a group in which someone consistently displayed self-oriented behaviour. What do you believe was the motivation behind it? How did it affect the group? Was it resolved and, if so, how?

What might have been done in the way of planning that could have anticipated and reduced the effect of the behaviour?

If you can, describe a situation in which self-oriented behaviour ultimately had a positive impact on a group (perhaps because it was resolved and the group benefited from that).

Finally, is there a general principle or guideline regarding self-oriented behaviour that you can draw from your examples?

If your conclusion is to the effect that all behaviour in a group is important, and even that which disrupts the group is worthy of consideration, you are getting the point. Nevertheless, persistent self-oriented behaviour in your group, like a knock in your car engine, is worth checking out before going much further.

At the risk of repetition, both agenda/task and process/-maintenance behaviours are important in most groups and persistent self-oriented behaviour should not go unchallenged. It is usually the manager's responsibility to ensure that an optimum mix of agenda/task and process/maintenance behaviour prevails.

A way to develop a more detailed picture of process in meetings is to use a more systematic approach to identifying agenda/task and process/maintenance behaviours. Next is the Self-diagnosis Checklist (Table 6.5). The left-hand column defines each of the three types of contribution that group members can make at a meeting – behaviours that focus on agenda/task, those that help the group keep its cohesion (process/maintenance) and self-oriented behaviours. The five columns to the right provide a means to indicate, by making ticks or check marks, your observations of the frequency of the different types of behaviour. Tick the columns that represent your own or other members' behaviour.

Review your responses to that checklist and make a note of your answers to these questions.

Are you, in general, an agenda/task-oriented or process/maintenance-oriented person? How would you account for your pattern? How much is conscious? How much is your 'personality'?

Table 6.5 *Self-diagnosis checklist*

Member	1	2	3	4	5
Agenda/task behaviours					
Suggesting new ideas					
Seeking information (asks for additional information)					
Giving information (offers facts or other information)					
Seeking opinion (seeks clarification and ideas)					
Elaborating (gives examples or explanations)					
Coordinating (links suggestions or ideas)					
Summarizing (pulls together ideas or suggestions)					
Testing feasibility (checks out solutions or ideas)					
Process/maintenance behaviours					
Encouraging (praises others and their ideas)					
Gatekeeping (brings in other people)					
Building agreement (proposes or agrees ways of working)					
Following (goes along with a group decision)					
Expressing group feeling (summarizes what the group is feeling)					
Both agenda/task and process/maintenance behaviours					
Testing for consensus (asks for group opinions on what is agreed)					
Mediating (works to settle differences in points of view)					
Relieving tension (uses humour to relax a period of tension)					
Using humour (uses humour to draw people together)					
Self-oriented behaviour					
Being agressive (shows hostility to the group or an individual)					
Blocking (slows the progress of the group by going off at a tangent)					
Going on (promotes own pet ideas or positions)					
Competing (vies with others)					
Seeking sympathy (looks for sympathy for one's problems)					
Special pleading (makes suggestions related to own concerns)					
Horsing around (clowns or disrupts)					
Attention seeking (calls attention to self by loud or aggressive talking or extreme ideas)					
Withdrawing (indifferent, daydreaming, wandering from the subject)					

Are there types of group or meeting in which you alter your 'normal' style? If so, describe these and suggest your reasons for changing.

Are you willing to try different patterns of behaviour in meetings in the future? If so, which ones? What results do you expect?

One of the keys to being a good manager in a group setting is to be aware when certain role behaviours are needed. For example, a group has been intensely involved in problem solving and kept their 'noses to the grindstone', but there is still a lot more to do. Instead of summarizing yet one more time in the hope of moving ahead, you say, 'It's been a long meeting and we all know there is further to go, but it seems a good time for a break'. You switch from agenda/task to process/maintenance behaviours. You might not finish as soon, but you will have a better-functioning group when you get back to the task.

Now that you are familiar with the Diagnosis Checklist and have applied it to your own group behaviour, you may find that using it, in the role of coach to selected groups you manage, can improve group functioning. Here are two useful exercises.

1   At a team meeting, distribute a blank copy of the Self-diagnosis Checklist, which can be found at the end of this chapter. Encourage discussion of it as a means of building more awareness in the team of what is involved in making

team meetings more effective. After each person has studied the checklist, ask them to discuss with the person next to them, for a few minutes, the three types of behaviour and their responses. Then have each person plan to employ one of their little used agenda/task or process/maintenance behaviours during the meeting. A few minutes prior to the end of the meeting, have the whole group discuss reactions to the exercise. Did it confirm their original beliefs? How did it feel to try new behaviours? How well balanced were agenda/task and process/maintenance group behaviours?

2 Use a blank copy of the checklist to observe the process of a meeting. Ignore the titles, using the space instead to make tally marks. Appoint an observer, or reporter, whose task it is to mark the type of behaviour after each contribution. Continue doing this for 10 minutes, then ask the observer to report the results. As the group reviews its results, ask the following questions to improve its understanding of its dynamics:

- 'Are we more agenda/task or process/maintenance oriented? Why?'
- 'Do we display many self-oriented behaviours? How does the group respond to them?'
- 'Based on the answers to these two questions, what speculations might we make about the functioning of the group?'
- 'What do we need to do to make our future meetings even more productive?'

Objectives and action plans

Reflect on this chapter and the learning for you. Collect together all your thoughts on your own performance. From this, set yourself one or two clear objectives from each section.

Objectives
To improve the effectiveness of the group dynamics in my meetings I will...

Build on your objectives and convert them into action plans.

Action plan
To achieve my objectives, I will...

How will you know when you have achieved your objectives?

I will review progress on (date three months ahead)

and on (date six months ahead)

Enter these dates in your diary.

This is perhaps an opportune time to carry out a more general review of what you have learned or achieved and what you have discovered about yourself. Return again to the objectives you had before you started reading this book and consider to what extent your thinking has altered.

As you apply your learning, remember that the aim is never to devise blueprints and then adhere to them rigidly. Rather, the key is continuous review to establish whether plans are working and, if they are not, to revise objectives and action plans in order to realize success. It is worth regularly setting time aside, perhaps on a monthly basis, to review progress in this way.

We hope that you have found the material in this book enjoyable, and that you have benefited from working through it and now feel confident that a smarter way of working is within your reach.

Who Talks?

Group member	Contributions	Total	Percent

Total

Who Talks? How Long?

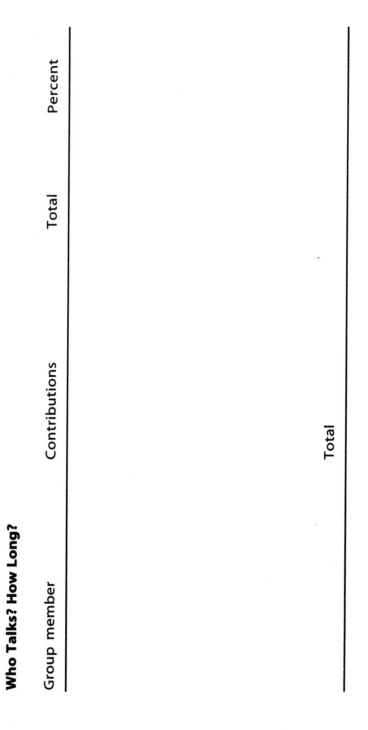

Group member	Contributions	Total	Percent
Total			

Who Interrupts Whom?

Name

Total

Total

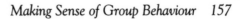

Who Talks? After Whom?

Name

Total

Self-diagnosis checklist

Member	1	2	3	4	5
Agenda/task behaviours					
Suggesting new ideas					
Seeking information (asks for additional information)					
Giving information (offers facts or other information)					
Seeking opinion (seeks clarification and ideas)					
Elaborating (gives examples or explanations)					
Coordinating (links suggestions or ideas)					
Summarizing (pulls together ideas or suggestions)					
Testing feasibility (checks out solutions or ideas)					
Process/maintenance behaviours					
Encouraging (praises others and their ideas)					
Gatekeeping (brings in other people)					
Building agreement (proposes or agrees ways of working)					
Following (goes along with a group decision)					
Expressing group feeling (summarizes what the group is feeling)					
Both agenda/task and process/maintenance behaviours					
Testing for consensus (asks for group opinions on what is agreed)					
Mediating (works to settle differences in points of view)					
Relieving tension (uses humour to relax a period of tension)					
Using humour (uses humour to draw people together)					
Self-oriented behaviour					
Being agressive (shows hostility to the group or an individual)					
Blocking (slows the progress of the group by going off at a tangent)					
Going on (promotes own pet ideas or positions)					
Competing (vies with others)					
Seeking sympathy (looks for sympathy for one's problems)					
Special pleading (makes suggestions related to own concerns)					
Horsing around (clowns or disrupts)					
Attention seeking (calls attention to self by loud or aggressive talking or extreme ideas)					
Withdrawing (indifferent, daydreaming, wandering from the subject)					

INDEX